Spiritual Growth Through the Gospel

# WHY JESUS?

## Exploring Relationship
## with Jesus
## in Matthew's Gospel

## Fr. David M. Knight

**His Way, Inc.**
**1310 Dellwood Avenue**
**Memphis, Tennessee 38127**
**901-357-6662**

Acknowledgements

I wish to give thanks to Sr. Mary Peter Rowland who
prayed me through this book and I think gave it to me
from God. I would also like to thank Sr. Mary Agnes Stretz
of the same Monastery of St. Clare in Memphis, Tennessee
for typing this book and encouraging me.

First American Edition 1981
Second printing 1987
Third printing 1994
Fourth printing 1997

# TABLE OF CONTENTS

# INTRODUCTION:

## THE GOOD NEWS OF A NAME

What could have inspired Matthew to headline his Gospel with a family tree? His first act in announcing to us the good news of our salvation is to supply us with a list of the names of Jesus' ancestors that stretches back forty-four generations! His Gospel begins:

> A family record of Jesus Christ, son of David, son of Abraham. Abraham was the father of Isaac, Isaac the father of Jacob, Jacob the father of Judah and his brothers.
>
> Judah was the father of Perez and Zerah, whose mother was Tamar.
> Perez was the father of Hezron,
> Hezron the father of Ram,
> Ram was the father of Amminadab,

and so on. This, as the first paragraph of the greatest news bulletin in the world, is hardly an attention-grabber!

We will see in chapter two how significant this beginning was for the Jews to whom Matthew was writing, and how significant it can be for us when we understand it. But just to get into the subject, let's reflect on what it means to us today that the story of Jesus Christ should begin with a list of individual, human names.

In the beginning, people related to God pretty exclusively in His role as God. He was the Creator, the Provider of life and all good things. He was also Lawgiver and Judge. It was generally taken for granted that those who lived right in this world would be blessed by Him with good crops, healthy children, happy homes, and a long life; while those who displeased Him would find both earth and sky turned against them. God was a good God, but what He wanted most of all was that this world and all the people in it should function as He created them to function. And anything that didn't function as it should tended to get destroyed.

People naturally assumed that if someone fell sick, died young, or happened to get caught in an earthquake, or if his business didn't go well, that person must have done something displeasing to God. And since God was great and mysterious, it wasn't always too clear just what pleased Him and what did not. People did a lot of guessing, and that's how superstition was born.

Then God spoke to Abraham. He chose Abraham and all of his descendants to be His special People. He formed an alliance with them. And for the first time in history He told people in very clear terms just exactly what pleased Him and what displeased Him. He dictated the Ten Commandments to Moses and gave His People the Law. From then on there was no need for guesswork. People knew what God would punish and what He would reward. There was still a lot of superstition about the *way* He punished and rewarded — people still thought the sickness and the earthquakes were sent by God against those who displeased Him — but a start had been made. With the Covenant and the Law the relationship between God and His People was at least on a definite basis.

At the same time, God told Moses His name.

This doesn't sound like anything special to us. For us a name is just a label we use to distinguish one person from another; something to call a person by. We have telephone books full of names, and we use people's names to look up practical things about them, like their credit ratings and addresses. But in the ancient world, and for the people of the Bible, a person's name was a very sacred thing. The person himself — his identity, his character, his individuality and specialness — was expressed in his name. To reveal your name to someone was to reveal your very self. It was to enter into relationship.

This is why Moses made such an issue over knowing God's name when the Lord appeared to him in the burning bush and wanted Moses to lead His People out of Egypt.

> "But," said Moses to God, "when I go to the Israelites and say to them, 'The God of your fathers has sent me to you,' if they ask me, 'What is his name?' what am I to tell them?"

Moses knew that if God would tell him His name, then the people would believe that Moses was really someone special to God, that God had chosen him and he could be trusted. And God kenw this too. So for the first time in history He revealed His name as YAHWEH, the name which means I AM:

> God replied, "I am who am." Then he added, "This is what you shall tell the Israelites: I AM sent me to you. . .

"This is my name forever;
this is my title for all generations." (*Exodus* ch. 3)

From that moment on, Moses knew that he was
God's "intimate friend" (see *Exodus* 33:11-12). And
when he asked God to give him further proof of His
friendship by revealing Himself even more deeply,
God responded with a vision of His glory during
which He pronounced to Moses His name:

> Then Moses said, "Do let me see your glory!" He
> answered, "I will make all my beauty pass before you,
> and in your presence I will pronounce my name,
> 'LORD'. . ."

The fact that Matthew begins his Gospel by
presenting to us the name of Jesus Christ in connection with a whole list of other individual, human
names is something to think about. It invites us to
think about the revelation of His name — of His
person — in our lives, and about the meaning our
own names — our own selves — have to Him. It
invites us to think about our personal relationship
with God.

Of all the things that we want most in life, it is
deep, intimate relationship with others, or at least
with some other person, that we ache for most
strongly. Ask yourself: would you rather be rich, or
have someone — a friend, husband or wife — who
really loves you, really understands you? What means
more to you: success, of someone to share it with?
Would you rather be healthy and alone, or handicapped but blessed with a perfect spouse?

What we want more than anything else on earth
is too know and love some other person with our
whole hearts, and to be known and loved completely
in return. If we have this, we can endure almost any

other deprivation. Without it, nothing else can make us happy anyway.

But how many people find a perfect friend? A perfect wife? A perfect husband?

Matthew's Gospel begins by announcing to us that there is one person who calls each of us by name — by our deepest, most personal names — and who invites us to know Him by His deepest, most personal name in return. In Jesus Christ God has drawn near to each one of us, extending His hand in friendship, opening His arms to embrace us to His heart.

The Gospel reveals that what God wants most of all is *not* that this world and all the people in it should function as He created them to function. What God wants most of all is *relationship*. He wants each of us to call Him and know Him by name as He calls each of us by name.

And Jesus was God's way of revealing this.

## CHAPTER ONE

## JESUS IS FRIENDSHIP WITH GOD

When we ask, "Why Jesus? What does Jesus mean to me? What should He mean?" the first answer we can give is "Love." Through Jesus the love of God for us, and our response of love to Him, can become a present, experienced reality. Jesus is the bridge of relationship. Through Him, and with Him we can have friendship with God.

The Father took the first step toward friendship with us by revealing His name to Moses and His Law to Israel, His chosen People. Because of His Covenant with the Jews, God stayed close to them. He "took up residence" in their midst in a special way — first in the Ark of the Covenant, then in that special section of the Temple called the "Holy of Holies." He spoke to them through Moses and the prophets. He intervened in their history, leading them out of Egypt and into the Promised Land, guiding their development, defeating their enemies, punishing them when they needed it, gradually preparing them, and the human race through them, to receive the revelation of His Son.

Because of God's special presence to Israel, because of his precise revelation to them and intervention in their history, Moses could say to his fellow Jews: "For what great nation is there that has gods so close to it as the LORD, our God, is to us whenever we call upon him? Or what great nation has statutes and decrees that are as just as this whole law which I am setting before you today? (*Deuteronomy* 4:7-8)

> Ask now of the days of old, before your time, ever since God created man upon the earth; ask from one end of the sky to the other: Did anything so great ever happen before? Was it ever heard of? Did a people ever hear the voice of God speaking from the midst of fire, as you did, and live? Or did any god venture to go and take a nation for himself from the midst of another nation, by testings, by signs and wonders, by war, with his strong hand and outstretched arm, and by great terrors, all of which the LORD, your God, did for you in Egypt before your very eyes? (*Deuteronomy* 4:32-34)

But all of this did not yet make possible true friendship with God: not that personal, intimate friendship with God as He is in His inmost self which the coming of Jesus made possible. Moses was called to be God's "intimate friend," but the goal of the Covenant was still very much to help people relate to God in His role as God. Moses himself drew this as a conclusion from the passage we have just cited: "All this you were allowed to see that you might know the LORD is God and there is no other." And the lesson that followed from it was: "You must keep his statutes and commandments . . . that you and your children after you may prosper. . . ." (*Deuteronomy* 4:35, 39-40)

When Jesus came, however, a new door opened between God and man. In Jesus — in His personality, His words, His actions, His behavior — we see God Himself revealed. Jesus is not the Law of God made flesh, the Law incarnate. He is the Person of God made flesh, God visible and revealed in human terms before our eyes. Jesus isn't God acting out a part, God pretending to be man in order to show us how to do it. If Jesus were just God "setting an example" for us in human terms, like a dramatics coach stepping into a role to show an actor how to play it, He would not be the revelation of God: just the revelation of how God wants us to behave as human beings.

But Jesus is God become man. What His words and actions reveal is the personality of God Himself. Not every word Jesus spoke was composed to be a lesson; not every action was calculated as an example. With those who lived and walked and talked with Him, Jesus was just Himself. They knew Him, not only as teacher and healer and Messiah, but just as Jesus. They came to know all sorts of things about His personality which were not relevant to "religion." (Unless, of course, you understand religion in the Christian sense of just knowing and loving God as He is — but that is precisely what Jesus made possible). Jesus was, in the most complete way, God dwelling among us; not just God acting for us, responding to our prayers, teaching, healing, saving; but God simply *being* among us — and being Himself — so that we might know Him and love Him as He is.

Jesus changed the nature of religion. Instead of religion being a set of things for people to believe and do in order to be pleasing to God, religion became simply friendship with God: — love, relationship, intimacy. For a Christian, to be "religious" does not mean just to keep all of God's laws; it means to know and love God as He is in Himself, and to respond to Him as to a friend. Christianity is a total relationship with God: God reveals everything He is to us (and not just the "religious" things according to the old meaning of the word) and we respond to God with love and service in everything we do, as to a friend (and not just in our "religious" acts, according to the old meaning).

What makes this relationship with God possible is His total revelation of Himself in Jesus. The difference between the self-revelation of God in the Old Testament and in the New is the difference between the exposure a person makes of himself at a press conference and at a party. In the Old Testament God granted formal interviews to Moses and the prophets, and He delivered official messages according to His role as God. In the New Testament God simply lives among His People, being Himself, responding according to His own character and personality to whatever is said and done around Him, just as we do. In the New Testament Jesus does speak officially as Teacher, as Savior and God. But the revelation of Himself is not limited to "official" occasions. At every moment and in every response He makes to life and to people He is simply among us, being Himself, letting Himself be known, inviting our love and showing us His own. And this is the key to our religion.

There may be some who at this point have a practical question: "How can my religion be today what you are describing? Jesus is not living among us now. I can't get to know Him the way I get to know the men and women I live and work with. Now that Jesus has ascended into heaven again, aren't we right back where we were before?"

An adequate answer to this question would take us beyond the scope of this present book, which only asks "*Why* Jesus?" and not "*How* do I get to know Him?" An adequate answer would take us into discipleship and an explanation of different kinds of prayer — prayer over the Scriptures, meditation, contemplation, and discernment prayer which teaches us to recognize His present action in our lives through inspirations and movements of the heart. It would take us into deeper explanation of how the Incarnation continues today: how Jesus continues to be among us in flesh and blood, interacting with us humanly, teaching, speaking and responding to us in human words and gestures (chapters five and six begin to deal with this). It is enough for us at this point, however, just to affirm the *fact* without teaching the *way*. And the fact is that Jesus came in order that through our relationship with Him, our human interaction with Him, we might come to know God as a person, and experience with God the fullness of warm, personal friendship that is the deepest desire of our souls. Or, as St. Paul puts it, that we might "grasp fully, with all the holy ones, the breadth and length and height and depth of Christ's love, and *experience* this love which surpasses all knowledge, so that you may attain to the fullness of God himself" (*Ephesians* 3:18-19).[1]

Even the declaration of this invitation would not be enough, however, if we did not add a word about the sending of the Holy Spirit. Our friendship with God is not like any other; it is made perfect by God's indwelling presence with us.

The problem in all human friendships is that our union with the other can never be perfect, just because we fall short of perfect communication. How many deeply loving married couples, truly united with each other in mind and heart and will, still suffer from areas of mutual misunderstanding? Try as we might, we do not seem able to make another understand just exactly what we think, feel, fear or desire. We often give up and stop trying.

If we could only just somehow move our minds over into the mind of our friend, and think our thoughts from within him; and shift our feelings over into his heart, so that he could experience them for himself, then we could be truly one. Then we would know we are understood as deeply as we understand ourselves. But we cannot do this.

God can, however. And when He sends us the Holy Spirit (which is really a way of saying that all three Persons — Father, Son and Spirit — come to dwell within us: see *John* 14:15-23), He literally sends His own mind and heart, His own thoughts, feelings and desires, into us. In the measure that we surrender ourselves to the Spirit who lives within us, letting Him enlighten us and guide us entirely by faith, hope and love, we share in the understanding God has of Himself, and in the love God has for Himself and for all creation. No unity can be deeper or more complete than this. The perfect joy of heaven is nothing but this same sharing in God's life brought to completeness without any obstacles to impede it.

This is the essence of eternal life. Jesus Himself said so:

> Eternal life is this: to *know you*, the only true God, and him whom you have sent, Jesus Christ. (*John* 17:3)

When we say that Jesus gives us "eternal life," we do not just mean that because of Jesus God allows us to live forever in some kind of perfect happiness after death. Life that never ends is *everlasting* life; but *eternal* life means life that has no beginning and no end; life that always was and always will be. Only God's life is eternal. To receive "eternal life," therefore, means to receive a share in the life of God

Himself. And God's life is that "fellowship" of mutual understanding and love that exists between the Father, the Son and the Spirit.

When we say that Jesus gives us "eternal life," therefore, we mean that through Jesus God has made it possible for us to *know God* here and now in a way that is the basis for real friendship. "Eternal life is this: to *know you*, the only true God, and Jesus Christ whom you have sent." Through Jesus, and through the Spirit He gives, we can share in that intimate knowledge of God which God has of Himself; that the Father, the Son and the Spirit have of each other. We can take part in the mutual understanding and love which unites the three Persons of the Blessed Trinity to one another. It is this that John was talking about when he wrote:

> . . . We proclaim to you the *eternal life* that was present to the Father and became visible to us. What we have seen and heard we proclaim in turn to you so that you may *share life* with us. This *fellowship* of ours is with the Father and with his Son, Jesus Christ. Indeed, our purpose in writing you this is that our joy may be complete. (1 *John* 1:2-4)

John began his Gospel by telling us that from all eternity God, knowing Himself, was whispering the word of His self-understanding: "God!" This Word of God's self-knowledge is God the Son, whom John just calls "the Word of God."

And it is this Word — which "was from the beginning," which became flesh and was revealed to us in Jesus Christ:

> The Word became flesh and made his dwelling among us, and we have seen his glory: the glory of an only Son coming from the Father, filled with enduring love. (*John* 1:14)

This Word, John says, is "what we proclaim to you:

> what was from the beginning,
> what we have heard,
> what we have seen with our eyes,
> what we have looked upon
> and our hands have touched —
> we speak of the word of life. (1 *John* 1:1)

This is what it really means, now that Christ has come, for us to know God's name. God doesn't pass before us in a mystical vision as He did with Moses on the mountain-top, crying out His name. Rather, He sends His Spirit into our hearts, the Spirit of Jesus who alone knows the Father and who is known by the Father alone (see *Matthew* 11:27), and His Spirit pronounces within our hearts the Word of God's name that is known only to God. He begins to utter within us that same Word of God's self-knowledge that God has been whispering from all eternity: the Word that was made flesh in Jesus.

And we share in the Spirit's utterance. We share in His act of knowing. With Him we also begin to breathe out our own divine word of knowledge: "Jesus!" We speak His name — not of ourselves, but in union with the Spirit who is speaking it from within our hearts. In the Spirit we cry out "Jesus!" in understanding of the Son, and "Abba!" in understanding of the Father (see 1 *Corinthians* 12:3 and *Romans* 8:15-16. See also *Revelation* 2:17 and 19:12-16).

When we know God's name, our own name changes. When God reveals His name to us, not only does He by that act enter into a new relationship with us — as Father, Friend, Indwelling Spirit — but we also enter into a new relationship with Him. We receive "a new name, pronounced by the mouth of the LORD" (*Isaiah* 62:2). We know ourselves to be different; that we have been changed, and changed in the deepest roots of our being, by the fact of being drawn into relationship with God.

We are a *"new creation"* (2 *Corinthians* 5:17), no longer slaves but sons (*Galatians* 4:7; *Romans* 8:14-16); called to live by the Spirit in freedom (*Galatians* 5:13 ff.); not in uncomprehending conformity to an external law, but in a way that is a willing, personal expression of new attitudes and values that are poured out in our hearts and written on our minds (*Hebrews* 10:14-16; *Romans* 5:6). We are *identified with Christ*. Through our union with Him we have put on a new identity, that of the Body of Christ on earth (*Romans* 12:1-5; 1 *Corinthians* 12:1-27). Each one of us is a new person, one who grows in knowledge as he is formed anew in the image of Christ and God (*Colossians* 3:10). We live now according to the mind of Christ (1 *Corinthians* 2:10; *Philippians* 2:5), because he dwells in our hearts through faith and strengthens us inwardly through the working of His Spirit (*Ephesians* 3:14 ff.).

We have that *assurance* which comes from our knowledge of the mystery of God revealed in Christ (*Colossians* 1:2-3). In Him the fullness of divinity resides in bodily form, and ours is a share in this fullness (*Colossians* 2:9). There was a time when we were darkness, but now we are light in the Lord and know ourselves to be children of light (*Ephesians* 5:8). We have been rescued from the power of darkness and brought into the kingdom of God's beloved Son. Through Him we have redemption and the forgiveness of our sins (*Colossians* 1:12-14). We have been accepted by Christ (*Romans* 15:7) and brought into oneness with Him (*Ephesians* 1:7-10, 22-23; and 2:11-12). We are co-heirs with Him of all the Father's riches, co-heirs with His chosen People, members of His Body, and sharers in all that God has promised (*Ephesians* 3:6). We have been consecrated in Christ (1 *Corinthians* 1:2), anointed and sealed with His Spirit (2 *Corinthians* 1:21-22). The Spirit has been deposited in our hearts like a "down payment" of future glory (2 *Corinthians* 1:22). Our names have been written in the book of the living (*Revelation* 3:5) because the name of Christ has been written on our hearts (*Revelation* 3:12; 14:1) — that is, because it has been given to us who know His name to know Him as He is (*Revelation* 22:4).

Knowing the name of Jesus *changes our own names*, because to know God as He is is to *become different in every way*. As St. Paul says, "All of us, gazing on the Lord's glory with unveiled faces, are being transformed from glory to glory into his very image by the Lord who is the Spirit" (2 *Corinthians* 3:18). This is the fruit of relationship with God.

Because we bear a new name and have entered into a new relationship with God, we know that it is God's will that we should *grow in holiness* (1 *Thessalonians* 4:3; 2 *Corinthians* 5:21; *Ephesians* 5:25-27). Our destiny and our call is to be made perfect as our heavenly Father is perfect (*Matthew* 5:48). Since we are now the Body of Christ on earth, it could not be otherwise.

All of this is the first answer we make to the question, "Why Jesus? What should He mean to me?" Jesus is for us the Person who invites us into intimate relationship with Himself, and so into intimate relationship with God. He invites us to let our names be written forever in association with His. Matthew began his Gospel — his account of the "good news" — by linking individual, human names, human persons, with the name of Jesus Christ. This is the way he began the good news, and this is the way the good news of Jesus begins for us.

### FOOTNOTE

[1]The way to attain to experienced knowledge of Christ is explained to some extent in my books *His Way* (St. Anthony Messenger Press, 1977) and *Lift Up Your Eyes To The Mountain* (Dimension Books, 1981).

## CHAPTER ONE: JESUS IS FRIENDSHIP WITH GOD — *Matthew* 1:1-16

*Summary:*

1. Throughout Jewish history, the more God revealed of Himself to people, the more He invited them into intimate, personal relationship with Himself.
2. In the Scriptures, a person's *name* expresses his inmost, personal reality. To know a person's name is to know what is unique and special about him. When we find Matthew beginning his Gospel by linking the name of Jesus with a list of human names, it invites us to reflect on the personal relationship each one of us is called to have with God through Jesus Christ.
3. In Jesus God reveals Himself to us, not just in His "role" as God — Creator, Lawgiver, Judge, etc. — but without reservations as a human being, a person externalized in flesh. Jesus' "role" as incarnate Savior was to be among us, being Himself — responding to life and to people around Him according to His own personality. It is knowing and responding to God as revealed in Jesus Christ that initiates our salvation.
4. The external revelation of God in Jesus is accompanied by an interior revelation by the Holy Spirit who speaks the "name" of the Father and of Jesus in our Hearts. We know Jesus both through his human words and actions, and through the light of the Spirit within us. This knowledge of Jesus makes us different, changes our "names."

*Questions for prayer and discussion:*

1. What do I feel (not think) is more important to God: me, or having law and order in the universe? Which is more important to my father? To my mother? Do I have more feeling of being loved by God or by my father? My mother? Why?

2. How important are personal relationships to me? Would I rather be rich or have close friends? Be admired by a lot of people or be loved by a lot of people? Be a success or have a happy marriage?

3. How important is it to me to have a personal relationship with God? Am I more concerned about keeping Him "on my side" (or keeping myself on His side), or about getting to know Him as a friend? When I check up on my religious performance, do I ask myself first whether I'm keeping the rules, or whether I'm becoming more intimate with God as a friend?

4. This chapter invites me to make use of Jesus. In what way? Have I decided to do this? Why? (If the answer is yes, *how* will I do it?)

## CHAPTER TWO

## JESUS IS MEANING IN LIFE

In the family tree of Jesus Matthew has hidden at least three clues to the theme of his whole Gospel. These clues are liable to be overlooked entirely by modern readers, because the style of history we are used to is plainspeaking and unimaginative. We read our history in the newspapers, and we don't look for crossword puzzles in the middle of the front-page story.

Not so the Jews of Matthew's time.

When Matthew wrote, the printing press had not yet been invented, of course; very few books were written; very few people could read them, and those who did write or read books were willing to devote a lot of time to the endeavor. For this reason, the writers could and did say many things so subtly that modern readers seldom notice them at all. They wrote their books like puzzles, and to understand them one had to be alert for clues.

Another reason for this was that their books were not intended for most people to read, but to hear. They were written to be read by the few who could read to the vast majority who could not. Consequently, when an author wanted to announce a new chapter, or a change of topic, he couldn't do it as we do, by putting a title in the middle of the page, or by indenting a new paragraph, because that would not appear to the listeners. Everything we do today by titles, subtitles, paragraphing and underlining or italics, the authors in biblical times had to do by weaving clues into the words of the text itself.

There is such a clue in the very first line of Matthew's Gospel. We may not have noticed it, but the first hearers of the Gospel would have spotted it at once. Matthew begins with the words, "A family record of Jesus Christ, son of David, son of Abraham. . . ."

That's the clue. Everyone knew that Abraham came before David in history; why does Matthew put David first in Jesus' family tree?

The answer is obvious — if you happen to be a first-century Jew accustomed to look for such things. The theme of Matthew's Gospel, from beginning to end, is going to be that Jesus is the promised "Son of David," which is one of the titles the Jews gave to the Messiah they were expecting.

In case anyone missed the first clue, Matthew gives another. He ends his listing of Jesus' family tree with the statement:

> Thus the total number of generations is:
> from Abraham to David, fourteen generations;
> from David to the Babylonian captivity, fourteen generations;
> from the Babylonian captivity to the Messiah, fourteen generations.

Now everyone knew that Matthew hadn't the slightest idea how many generations there actually were between Abraham and Jesus. Such records did not exist. And even if they had existed, what would be the point of listing every ancestor Jesus had, all the way back to Abraham? So Matthew's first listeners caught on right away that he was giving them another clue. Why fourteen generations? Why repeat it three times?

Every letter in the Jewish alphabet had a number assigned to it, much in the way that we, as children, used to play at writing code messages to each other by making "A" equal one, "B" two, and so on. According to the Jewish system, the letters in the name "David," which was written DVD, without any vowels, added up to fourteen. By dividing Jesus' ancestors into three groups of fourteen, Matthew is making the point again that Jesus is the Son of David, and that this is what his Gospel is going to tell us about him.

We may tend to get exasperated at this point and throw the Gospel down in favor of a crossword puzzle. But Matthew's hearers didn't have crossword puzzles, so they got the same fun out of working out the clues in the Gospel. Besides, once you work out something like this you tend to remember it. And what Matthew said about Jesus, he wanted people to remember.

There was always the chance, of course, that some of Matthew's listeners might not have known what the title "Son of David" really meant. They may not have recalled the promise God made to King David through the prophet Nathan, that He would give David a son, an heir, who would sit on David's throne, and through whom the kingship of David would last forever. (See 2 *Samuel* 7:8-16).

So Matthew put in another clue — this one a clue both to the identity of Jesus and to the meaning and value that His title "Son of David" has for our lives. He divided the ancestors of Jesus into three groups. The first group covers the time from Abraham to

David; that is, from the beginning of Israel's history
as the chosen People until the high point of their
political and religious greatness under King David.
The second group reaches from David to the Babylonian captivity, or from the highest to the lowest
point in Jewish history. And the third group extends
from the Babylonian captivity to the birth of Jesus,
which gives us the clue we are looking for: Matthew
is saying that in Jesus Jewish history reaches its high
point again, that He is the "second peak" of Israel's
history, the long-awaited "second David," the Messiah. And since Jesus is the Son of David whose reign
is to last forever, in Him the history of Israel reaches a
height from which it will never decline. Jesus is the
final goal, the everlasting culmination of Jewish
history.

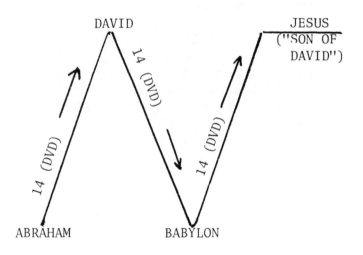

JESUS: "SON OF DAVID" AND PEAK OF
JEWISH HISTORY

Jewish history, however, is simply the truth of all human history revealed. Through His dealings with one nation, the Jews, God revealed His attitude, His love, His intentions with regard to the whole human race. And that is why Jesus as "Son of David" is significant to us.

The history of Israel and of God's dealings with Israel is the key to our own history. It reveals to us the divine orientation of all human evolution and development. Through His interventions in and guidance of Jewish history, God revealed to us His basic plan for the salvation of the human race. And it is in Jesus that this revelation becomes complete. Jesus is the final piece in the puzzle which makes the whole pattern appear. He is the cornerstone of the building, the keystone of the arch. (See *Matthew* 21:42; *Ephesians* 2:20; 1 *Peter* 2: 4-10). Only through Jesus do all the pieces fit together and make sense. Only through Him can we see the unity and intelligibility of the whole picture.

What Matthew is telling us is that all human history finds its meaning, its value, its intelligibility, in Jesus Christ. All the events in this world, great and small, have only one real purpose and value: to lead to Jesus Christ.

Quite simply, Jesus is the goal of human history. But what does this mean?

It is easy for us to see that Jesus was the goal of *Jewish* history. The real purpose of everything that took place during the history of Israel was to prepare the Chosen People and the world for the coming of Jesus. The life of every Jew who lived before Jesus took on special meaning and value from that fact. This relationship to Jesus, whether recognized or not, gave eternal significance to the name, to the life, and to the activities of every person in Israel. They were all, in some way, His "family tree."

But now that Jesus has come, how can He still be the goal of human history? A goal is something that has not yet been attained, something you work for. A goal is something you try to reach (like learning French) or try to bring into existence (like having a baby or building a house). How is Jesus a goal? He has already come to earth and redeemed the world. At most we might say He *left* us a goal: a teaching and example to live up to, a level of holiness and love we should try to reach. And if we are faithful He will give us the everlasting joy of heaven. We might say that heaven is our goal, or that being united in love with God forever is our goal. But can we say that *Jesus* (God-made-man, God in human flesh) is the goal of all human history in the sense that all human life, activity and events have as their purpose just one thing: to bring Jesus Christ into existence?

Yes, that is what the Scriptures teach us. Our lives, and our time on earth, have this enormous value: that we can spend them bringing Jesus Christ into existence.

To understand this we have to understand three things:

— First, we have to understand how the life of every Jew in Israel contributed in some way to making Jesus Christ who He was.

— Secondly, we have to understand what we are talking about when we say that Jesus will "come again." (It doesn't just mean that the Jesus who went away will come back).

— Thirdly, we have to understand how our lives and actions on earth — that is, the choices and decisions we make — will determine in some way or another what Jesus will be when He returns.

If we can understand these three things, we will know what it means to say that Jesus is the goal of all human history, and that the great value of our lives lies in the fact that we are called to bring Him into existence.

Then we will have answered again the question, "Why Jesus? What should He mean to me?" The answer will be, "Jesus is the only true purpose of my life; bringing Him to be is the only thing I can do that will have meaning and value forever." We will then appreciate Jesus as the one who gives purpose, direction and significance to our lives.

The first thing we have to look at is how the life of every Jew who lived before Jesus contributed to making Jesus who He was.

When we say "Jesus" we are speaking about a divine person — the Second Person of the Blessed Trinity, God the Son — who always was God and who became man. The mystery is that God the Son didn't *change* His nature — stop being God and start being man — but simply took a human nature to Himself, body and soul, and went on being the same divine Person He was, but with two natures. No new person was created or began to exist when God became man. The person we know as Jesus is God the Son, the Second Person of the Blessed Trinity, who has existed from all eternity.

The human nature of Jesus did begin to exist, however, when God took flesh in the womb of Mary. And when we speak of the "human nature" of Jesus this includes, not just His body, but a lot of things that we call "personality," which can be confusing. The *person* of Jesus is a divine person, God the Son. No new human person came to be when God the Son took a human nature to Himself at the Incarnation.

But the *personality* of Jesus was determined by a lot
of elements that came from His human nature, such
as His psychology, His cultural conditioning, certain
character traits and spontaneous patterns of reaction,
and the like. Hence the person people knew as Jesus
was not simply God in a human skin; that person was
also a Jew, of the first-century, from a country town,
with a particular family background and a lot of
personal experiences that shaped His outlook and
feeling about things as He grew up.

The point is that the total reality of Jesus, God
and man, was shaped and determined to a great
extent by the family he descended from, by the culture
He was part of, by the country He grew up in, by all
the history of human actions and decisions which
helped form His environment. His humanity was
shaped, just as ours is, by the world into which He
was born, and by all the human choices which, over
the course of centuries, helped to make that world
what it was. Jesus took flesh in the womb of a virgin,
but not in a virginal world. That world was then, as it
is today, the fruit of millions of human seeds. And so
is every man or woman who is born into it.

This is why Matthew's choice to begin his Gospel
with Jesus' family tree is so significant. By empha-
sizing the fact that the humanity of Jesus was the
product of a long line of ancestors he invites us to
reflect on the effect that every human life lived in this
world has on every other. To be human is to enter
into the solidarity of the human race. And what the
human race is at any given moment is determined, not
only by the free choices of the living, but by all the
free choices of those who have gone before them.
When God Himself was born into the tribe of Israel,
His reality as a human being was determined to some

extent by everyone who preceded Him.

When Jesus comes again at the end of time, what will His humanity consist of then? Will Jesus come back just as He was when He ascended into heaven, or do we mean something more than this when we speak of the "second coming of Christ"?

When Jesus comes again it will mean that everything God wanted to accomplish through the creation of the world is complete. It will mean that the redemption of mankind is complete: that redemption which Jesus accomplished on the cross, and which is now being extended to the whole world through the work and activity of all who are members of Christ's Body on earth.

What is this redemption?

We too quickly define redemption, or salvation, as just "getting to heaven," as if our whole lives on earth were just examination papers to be torn up and thrown away once we receive a passing grade. We speak of heaven as if it were a big stadium in which all are made happy by "seeing God." In such a heaven the only enduring effect our earthly lives of choices, decisions and self-determination have on our continuing existence is to determine, first of all, that we get there, and secondly, how close to the action we get to sit. The holy people get "front seats" or "high places" in heaven; the not-so-holy see God from the balcony or sit in the "lowest" places. But everything we have written on our exam papers is thrown away; only the grade remains.

According to this picture it would appear that the only reason God had for creating the universe was to get people into heaven. The whole cosmos, with all of its billions of years of evolution and development, and all of the human drama that has taken place throughout its history, are nothing but a launching platform. Once the population has been successfully lifted into orbit, the world and all that happened in it can be forgotten; it ceases to exist.

This picture is not true to the Scriptures, of course. Compare it with this mysterious passage from St. Paul. He is talking about the role of Jesus, both before the world was created, and after creation is brought to its fulfillment:

> He is the image of the Invisible God, the *first-born* of all creatures. *In him* everything in heaven and on earth was created, things visible and invisible . . . all were created through him, and *for him.* . . . In him *everything continues in being.* It is he who is *head of the body*, the church; he who is the *beginning*, the firstborn of the dead, so that *primacy may be his in everything.* It pleased God to make *absolute fullness* reside in him and, by means of him, to *reconcile everything in his person*, both on earth and in the heavens, making peace through the blood of his cross. (*Colossians* 1:15-20)

We may not understand this passage (which is normal, since it deals with the very mystery itself of God's intention in creation and redemption), but there are some points in the passage we should notice:

First, Jesus is the focus of creation itself. When God created the universe Jesus, or the incarnation of God in human flesh, was already somehow the goal. "All were created . . . *for him.*" Jesus is the "Alpha and the Omega, the First and the Last, the Beginning and the End" (*Revelation* 22:13). We will see later what this means.

Secondly, when Jesus died and rose from the dead, this was not the end of redemption, but in some way the "beginning." "He . . . is the beginning, the first-born of the dead. . . ." There is something still unfinished about redemption, something that needs to be brought to completion. The God who came in Jesus is a God who is still to come (see *Revelation* 1:1-8 and ch. 21-22).

Finally, the human incarnation of God in Jesus is meant to continue forever, but in such a way that all of creation is somehow drawn into this unity of God in human flesh which is Jesus. "*In him* everything continues in being . . . he is *head of the body. . . .*"

The final state of the world, and the glorification of all things which God had in mind from the beginning is a mystery of oneness: the unification of all creation "in Christ." "It pleased God to make *absolute fullness* reside *in him*, and by means of him to reconcile everything *in his person. . . .*"

St. Paul said the same thing in another place when he wrote:

> God has given us the wisdom to understand fully the mystery, the plan he was pleased to decree in Christ, to be carried out in the fullness of time; namely, to *bring all things in the heavens and on earth into one* under Christ's headship. (*Ephesians* 1:9-10)

This was God's intention from "before the world began" — that Jesus should "create in himself one new man," not only by uniting the Jews and the Gentiles in himself, but by bringing "all things in the heavens and on earth into one" within the unity of His Body, with Jesus as head (see *Ephesians* 2:11-22).

We may be tempted to think of this as being some kind of merely intentional unity: the unity that exists between a group of people who think alike, work together, have a common commitment, and follow the directions of a single leader. We interpret "under Christ's headship" as if it meant nothing more than "under His leadership," or under His authority, the way we speak of the "headship" of a chief of state or president of a corporation.

But Paul means more than this. There is no "mystery" to announce in the fact that God wants everyone to obey Jesus and follow His teachings. Paul would hardly call such a message "that mystery hidden from ages and generations past but now revealed to his holy ones." When Paul says, "God has willed to make known . . . the glory beyond price which this mystery brings to the Gentiles — the mystery of *Christ in you*, your hope of glory" (*Colossians* 1:26-27) he is talking about a mystery of oneness with Christ and in Christ which is similar to the unity that makes the cells of a body one with each other and with their head. We are "in Christ" the way cells are in the body by which they live; and Christ is "in us" the way a person is in his own body. With Christ, as members of His Body on earth, we form "one new man" (*Ephesians* 2:15). And as the life of Christ is extended to more and more members of the human race, and in each one grows to its fullness, *Christ* grows to "full stature" (*Ephesians* 4:13).

This is our real work in life and the reason for all the years we spend on earth, growing in grace ourselves and helping others to grow: we are all called to "roles of service for the faithful to *build up the body of Christ*, till we become one in faith and in the knowledge of God's Son, and *form that perfect man who is Christ come to full stature*" (*Ephesians* 4:12-13).

This Jesus is the Alpha and the Omega, the Beginning and the End. It was the vision of all of redeemed humanity united "in Christ" as His Body which inspired God to create the world in the first place. And this union of God and of all humanity "in

Christ" is the goal and final end of our redemption:

> He has put all things under Christ's feet and has made him, thus exalted, head of the church, *which is his body*: the *fullness* of him who fills the universe in all its parts." (*Ephesians* 1:22-23)

This is what creation and redemption are all about. This is what Paul was sent to preach: "the mystery of Christ, unknown to men in former ages but now revealed by the Spirit . . . the mysterious design which for ages was hidden in God, the Creator of all" (see *Ephesians* 3:4-11). This mysterious, real unity of all men and of all creation "in Christ" is the fulfillment of all history and the goal and purpose of every human existence.

When Jesus comes again at the end of time it will be, not only Jesus Himself, the Head of the Body, who comes, but the "whole Christ": Jesus Head and members. The "whole Christ," or "Christ come to full stature" will be Jesus plus all the human beings, men and women, who have been reborn by grace, incorporated as members into His Body, brought to light and to life by the gift of His Spirit. And the purpose and privilege of our lives is to help bring this "fullness of Christ" into being.

How do we do this? What is our contribution to this final reestablishment of all things in Christ? How can we help to bring the "whole Christ" into being?

In a word, our contribution lies in what we become ourselves and help others to become.

When Jesus comes again He will be, as He was at His Incarnation, God united to human nature. But at His second coming Jesus will be united, not only to His own human nature, the body and soul He was born with, but also to the human natures of all those who have been born again as members of His Body through baptism. The humanity of the "whole Christ" will include all those men and women who accepted to die "in Christ" in order that He might live again in them: who gave their bodies to be the Body of Christ, their flesh to Him for the life of the world. The "whole Christ" is Jesus the Head plus all of His members. And it is this reality of His total humanity, of His redeemed Body, that we are called to help create.

The first way we do this is simply by accepting to be and to grow as His body on earth. St. Paul exhorted the early Christians: "*Offer your bodies* as a living sacrifice holy and acceptable to God" (*Romans* 12:1). This was an exhortation to baptism and to all that it implies. Jesus needs and asks us to be His Body on earth. And the gift that each one of us makes to Jesus of his or her own individual humanity is a gift that no other can give Him.

Jesus needs to live in each one of us as we are. He doesn't need any exact physical or cultural duplicates of His own human nature. He has already shown what God would be in a humanity like His own: in the body and personality of Jesus of Nazareth, a first-century Jew with his own particular background, cultural conditioning and personal experience of life. Jesus, so far as we know, was healthy; He needs to reveal now what He would be as a person in poor health, as an invalid, as handicapped. Jesus was a man; He needs to show what He would be as a woman. Jesus was olive-skinned like the Mediterranean peoples; He needs to show what He would be as black, as white, as yellow and red. When He asks us, through St. Paul, to "offer our bodies as a living sacrifice to God," He is asking us to let Him reveal Himself and be present to the world in and through the uniqueness of our own bodies and personalities.

He is asking us to let Him live and act and express Himself in the unique, individual human nature and psychology that belongs to each one of us, with all of its unduplicated and unduplicatable characteristics.

And when Jesus comes again in His glory, that glory will be the glory of God shining through the human natures of all who have joined themselves to Him as His Body. We will be His glory (*John*, ch. 17), and He will be ours (*Colossians* 1:27).

We also contribute to the glory of the Jesus who will come again by helping others to give themselves to Him, or to give themselves more fully, so that He might live in all humanity without hindrance or restriction.

Our call of grace is to take part in Christ's mission, which is to "bring all things in the heavens and on earth into one under Christ's headship" (see *Ephesians* 1:9-10). This is a work of bringing every human institution, attitude and activity into harmony with the values preached by Jesus, with the dignity and destiny of the human race that He revealed. This is what it means to establish the Kingdom of God on earth and to be "fishers of men." And this is what it means to "build up the body of Christ" (*Ephesians* 4:12) until all of humanity forms, with Jesus its Head, "that perfect man who is Christ come to full stature" (*Ephesians* 4:13).

St. Paul characterized this as a work of reconciliation for the establishment of *peace* on earth.

Because our goal is to "bring all things into one under Christ's headship," a primary concern of every Christian is to bring about peace through reconciliation: peace between individuals and God; between nations and races; between social classes and ethnic groups;   between political   factions and business competitors; between religious denominations, warring philosophies and rival schools of thought; between men and women, the young and the old, parents and children, husbands and wives, and people who just don't like one another. This peace is not a suppression of all differences, but a reconciliation between persons. It is a healing of divisions through love, which does not depend on our overcoming all differences, either through persuasion or through power.

Christians are called to work at peace and reconciliation between people everyplace we are: at home, in our schools, on our jobs, in our social life, in our civic and political activities. In everything we do, the increase of love upon earth should be our goal.

This is not a work we attempt by our own power as human beings. It is God's work. It was begun, and it is being carried on through us today, by God, "who has reconciled us to himself through Christ and given us the ministry of reconciliation" (see 2 *Corinthians* 5:18-19).

This is a work of reconciling the human race into one *community* of mutual respect, understanding and love. This is what St. Paul sees the mission of the Church to be: to bring diverse individuals, peoples and cultures into relationship with each other and with God by uniting them "in Christ." It is a major theme of his letters.

St. Paul preaches that one great obstacle to this unity is the "law." By this he means, not the Ten Commandments or an insistence on morality, but the effort by any group to impose its own cultural expressions of devotion on others — even within the same Church. In his letters it is the Jewish or Mosaic law which he talks about specifically, because that was the "barrier" Paul himself had to work against in his efforts to unite Jewish Christians and Gentile con-verts.[1] But what he says about Christ breaking down this barrier and calling the Jews and Gentiles into unity applies to every other barrier and division that exists within the human race:

> But now in Christ Jesus you who once were far off have been brought near through the blood of Christ. It is he who is our peace, and who made the two of us one by breaking down the barrier of hostility that kept us apart. In his own flesh he abolished the law with its commands and precepts, to create in himself one new man from us who had been two and to make peace. . . . He came and "announced the good news of peace to you who were far off, and to those who were near"; through him we both have access in one Spirit to the Father. (*Ephesians* 2:13-18)

The vision that St. Paul holds up to inspire Christians in their work of carrying on the mission of Christ is one of unity and peace.

This unity is not of human making. It is not brought about through eloquence or "the persuasive force of 'wise' argumentation"; much less by military conquest and the forceful impositon of laws. It de-pends on the free response of people to the "convinc-ing power of the Spirit" (see 1 *Corinthians* 2:1-5). It is a unity only God can bring about, althouth He does it through the instrumentality of men. It is a work of the Spirit embodied in a community of flesh and blood. And this unity, this "blessed vision of peace," is the goal that Christianity holds up to the world:

> This means that you are strangers and aliens no longer. No, you are fellow citizens of the saints and members of the household of God. You form a build-ing which rises on the foundation of the apostles and prophets, with Christ Jesus himself as the capstone.

> Through him the whole structure is fitted together
> and takes shape as a holy temple in the Lord; in him
> you are being built into this temple, to become a
> dwelling place for God in the Spirit. (*Ephesians*
> 2:19-22)

Why Jesus? Because Jesus is the only true goal of
human history. The destiny which brings into focus
every life and every existence on earth is the reconciliation of all creatures with God and with one
another in the unity of the Body of Christ. And everything that we can do to help any person — including
ourselves — to live more fully "in Christ" will contribute to the everlasting reality which that Body will
be.

As "Son of David" Jesus is the second peak of
Jewish history, the goal of all human history, and He
provides a focus for everything we strive to do during
life. In this way He gives eternal signficance to our
names, which, as we write them by our choices and
decisions during life, are being written into the "family tree" of the Christ who is to come.

### FOOTNOTE

[1]The "law" St. Paul refused to impose on Gentile converts in-
cluded all the rules, rituals and customs of the Jewish way of life,
in which both their religion and their culture or national identity
found expression. Until Paul forced the leadership of the Church
to confront this issue (see *Galatians* ch. 2; *Acts*, ch. 15), it never
occurred to the first Christians — who were all Jews — that
anyone could be a follower of Jesus without converting to
Judaism and to all of its laws and practices. When the Church
decided, in the first Council of Jerusalem (*Acts*, ch. 15), not to
require Gentile Christians to keep the Jewish law, the barrier was
broken down and Christianity became a "catholic" religion; that
is, one not identified with any particular culture or cultural
expression of devotion.

CHAPTER TWO: JESUS IS MEANING IN LIFE —
*Matthew* 1:17

*Summary:*

1. The dividing of the names in Jesus' family tree into three groups of fourteen (the number for DVD), which takes us up from Abraham to David, down from David to Babylon, and up again to Jesus, is Matthew's way of introducing Jesus as the promised "Son of David." In Him God is at work in the world, intervening in human history to bring about the kingship of Christ over all creation. To cooperate with God in this work is the only way to contribute authentically to the true progress of the human race.

2. Jesus is the peak and goal of Jewish history. But Jewish history is the truth of all human history revealed. Thus Jesus (who came and who will come again) is presented here as the goal and fulfillment of all human life and activity. Our names are written forever in the book of the living (see *Revelation* 3:5) as His "family tree." What gives eternal meaning and value to any human name (any human lifetime) is to contribute in some way to the "fullness of Christ" — that is, to the union of all men with Jesus and the re-ordering of all human activities and institutions according to the attitudes and values He teaches.

3. Our human natures, joined to His, constitute the fullness of Christ's humanity. Hence we bring Jesus to "full stature" by giving ourselves entirely to Him as His Body on earth and by helping others to do the same.

4. A particular and special aspect of Christ's redemptive mission is the *reconciliation* of all things in Himself. Therefore we are particularly charged to be ministers of peace and reconciliation, calling all men and women on earth together into one community of mutual acceptance and love "in Christ."

*Questions for prayer and discussion:*

1. How do I think of "progress"? In what direction am I helping my country (my world) to develop? What meaning or value will the work I am doing still have a hundred years from now?

2. What is the difference between seeing Jesus (and religion) as *contributing* to progress, and seeing Jesus (and relationship with Him) as the *goal* of all human progress? How is my life contributing to the "reestablishment of all things in Christ"? What do I do that is a work of *reconciliation*?

3. What meaning does my knowledge of Jesus Christ add to my life? To the work I do? To my social relationships? To my civic obligations (paying taxes, voting, etc.)? To my family life? What meaning can it add?

4. This chapter invites me to work toward bringing Jesus Christ into fullness of existence through what I *become* and through what I *do*. What decisions will I make in response to this invitation? Why?

## CHAPTER THREE

## JESUS IS DELIVERANCE FROM SIN

Probably the first thought that comes to mind when we say, "Why Jesus?" is, "He is Savior." And this is the very next thing we read in Matthew's Gospel. The story of Christ's birth (*Matthew* 1:18-25) emphasizes three things:

— that Jesus has no earthy father; God is His Father;
— that He is to be called "*Jesus*," a name which means "God saves" or "The Lord is salvation";
— that He will be "*Emmanuel*," which means "God is with us."

In other words, Jesus, true son of Mary and true Son of the Father, is both man and God. He is God dwelling in our midst ("Emmanuel"). And He has come to save us. He is the *saving presence of God* among us.

We have already seen two ways in which Jesus "saves" our existence: He saves us from the essential *loneliness* of existence by inviting us into *personal relationship* — into friendship — with God in Himself. And He saves us from the *meaninglessness* of life by revealing to us the *goal of human history*, the purpose of creation, and our own part in bringing to

realization the final, complete oneness of all creatures
with God and with one another in Him. Now Matthew invites us to look at another way Jesus saves us:
"You are to name him Jesus because he will *save his
people from their sins*" (v. 21).

What does it mean to be saved from sin?

To answer this question, we first have to ask
what "sin" is. For most of us "sin" probably means
some specific action, our own free choice, which is
bad and which makes us guilty. Because of certain
free decisions we have made to do what is wrong —
our sins — we take it for granted that God is angry
with us, or displeased anyway, and will punish us.

I am not denying this explanation of sin. It does
go to the heart of what sin is: a free choice to do
wrong. And it may be the only explanation we were
capable of understanding when, as little children, we
were taught about sin. But if we say no more than we
have said, our understanding of sin as adults will be
both inadequate and misleading. The result of this
will be a misunderstanding about God which will
make it hard for us to relate to Him, and a misunderstanding about Jesus as Savior which will keep us
from appreciating Him as we should.

If we see no more in sin than an act which makes
us guilty, then we will see no more in salvation than
an act which grants us forgiveness. We sinned once
and lost the friendship of God; Jesus died once and
won it back for us. Or we have sinned many times,
and each time that we repent God forgives us because
of the sacrificial death of Jesus. Either way we look at
it, Jesus is not continuously saving us. He came once,
or He comes and goes as we have need. If salvation is
just pardon for sins, we can speak of Christ's saving
*interventions* in our lives, but not of His saving

*presence.* We might even say that now, having won forgiveness for us once-and-for-all on the cross, Jesus as Savior is a has-been! Once the lifeguard has pulled us out of the water and we have thanked him we don't need to relate to him as lifeguard anymore.

But the reality of sin as we experience it is not limited to isolated acts of free choice. These acts, it is true, are the only things which make us guilty. But there is in us something constant, something abiding, which we recognize as *sinfulness.* We don't love as we should; we have distorted attitudes and values; we are more self-centered than generous; we are enticed by things we are ashamed of. Even if we never choose, in any concrete, specific free act, to do what is wrong, nevertheless we know that the weight of *what we are* is always holding us down, keeping us from acting on the level of generosity and love we would desire.

The root meaning of the word used for "sin" in the Scriptures (*hamartia*) is "to miss" — to miss the mark, to fall short. And we keep falling short of the ideal, or missing the mark of perfect response, perfect choices, because there is so much within us, so much that is a part of what we are, which holds us back, drags us down, deflects us.

The ancient spiritual writers, in an effort to get specific about this weight of sinfulness within us, so that we could do something practical about it, identified seven roots of evil in us. They called them seven "capital sins" — meaning, not that these are specific sins in themselves, but seven *headings* under which sins can be classified. These are the roots; the sins that proceed from them are the fruits. The roots remain; the fruits come and go. The roots do not make us guilty; only our free choices — the fruits which spring from these roots in the form of concrete actions —

make us guilty. But the roots are always at work in us, trying to bear their fruits, sapping the energy that would otherwise go into good activity, weighing down our wills and distorting our perceptions through the fears and desires they generate.

These roots are traditionally identified as *pride, anger, envy, greed, lust, laziness* and *gluttony.* And they are understood to be *destructive* tendencies in us. They are not to be confused with their legitimate, healthy counterparts: a good self-image (which is not pride); healthy anger (which is not destructive); energizing desire for achievement, recognition, or love (which is not envy); normal attraction to wealth and possessions (which is not greed); spontaneous sexual desire (which is not lust); or an ordinary delight in comfort, rest or food (which is neither laziness nor gluttony). What we call the "capital sins" or roots of evil in ourselves are all *wounded* tendencies in our being, destructive tendencies, natural desires or drives that have gone awry and are no longer pointed toward their legitimate, healthy goals. They are not only the roots of sin in us; they are also the *effects* of sin — not just of our own sins, but of the sins of the world. They are a woundedness bequeathed to us by every previous member of mankind.

Every generation that has preceded us has helped make this world the environment that it is. We and our contemporaries are making it right now the environment it is for one another and the environment it will be for those who come after us. And much of what we are creating is destructive. By our sins we poison the environment we and others must live in.

I am not speaking here about the chemical poisons we inject into earth and air and water. I am speaking about the poisons we inject into one another when our behavior is destructive. How much have the exploitative words and actions of human beings over the ages contributed to turning spontaneous sexual desire into lust? How much of what we call "competitiveness" is really envy or greed, having become a destructive compulsion in us through the influence of countless words and actions great and small, dating back to the beginnings of the human race? As human beings we interact with one another; and as we do so, we affect one another. We mutually condition each other's thinking, feeling and behavior, sometimes in ways we are unable to reverse. Our sins leave their mark — both on individuals and on the culture. Like some of the substances which our industrial society is injecting into the atmosphere, or burying in the earth, or littering the sea floor with, our sins just hang around forever. They don't dissolve. They accumulate and poison the environment.

None of us escapes the influence of this environment. Before we are old enough to be guilty of any personal act of sin, destructive tendencies are formed within us, and destructive patterns of behavior, misguided ways of coping with the environment, have already become part of our personalities. Before we are old enough to know right from wrong we have become adept at responding to the aggressive, manipulative behavior of other people with aggressive, manipulative tactics of our own. We were born into the middle of a catfight, and we find ourselves scratching and clawing in self-defense even before our eyes are open.

Who will deliver us from this sin? — from the "sin" that is not an act of personal guilt, but rather the sinful, destructive effect in us of millions of years of accumulated human action and interaction on earth,

increased and intensified by the destructive activity of
the men and women around us and by our own free
and unfree destructive responses to our environment?

St. Paul was intensely aware of our need for
salvation from sin on this level. He cried out in his
letter to the Romans:

> I am weak flesh sold into the slavery of sin. I cannot
> even understand my own actions. I do not do what I
> want to do but what I hate . . . the desire to do good is
> there but not the power. . . . My inner self agrees with
> the law of God, but I see in my body's members
> another law at war with the law of my mind; this
> makes me the prisoner of the law of sin in my
> members.

And Paul concludes as we do: "What a wretched
man I am! Who can free me from this body under the
power of death?" (*Romans* 7:14-24).

The answer is Jesus — but not Jesus understood
only as the Savior who died on the cross two thousand years ago and won us pardon. The Jesus in
whom we find salvation from the sin that is a "law of
our members," the sin that conditions our very being
because we are a physical part of this universe, influ-
encing and influenced by everything in it, is a Jesus
who remains with us. He is the Jesus whose members
we become, and the law of whose members is His own
Spirit. St. Paul continues:

> There is no condemnation now for those who are in
> Christ Jesus. The law of the spirit, the spirit of life in
> Christ Jesus, has freed you from the law of sin and
> death. . . . Those who are in the flesh cannot please
> God. But you are not in the flesh; you are in the spirit,
> since the Spirit of God dwells in you. . . . If the Spirit
> of him who raised Jesus from the dead dwells in you,
> then he who raised Christ from the dead will bring
> your mortal bodies to life also through his Spirit
> dwelling in you.

We are debtors, then, my brothers — but not to the flesh, so that we should live according to the flesh. If you live according to the flesh, you will die; but if by the spirit you put to death the evil deeds of the body, you will live. (*Romans* 8:1-13)

To appreciate what Paul is saying here we have to understand three things:

— First, it is because we have *bodies* that we affect and are affected by our environment. All the woundedness that is in us from the accumulated sin of mankind is due to the fact that we are beings of flesh and blood, in physical contact with our environment and other people. This is why Paul speaks of "this body under the power of death." (Paul uses the word "death" to mean both spiritual death — sin — and physical death. The meanings are interchangeable, since only sin makes physical death an evil. Delivered from sin, we live forever in Christ and death has no power over us ).

— Secondly, when Paul speaks of "living according to the flesh," he means living according to the destructive tendencies programmed into us as a result of our contact with this world. To be "in the flesh" in this sense means to be a slave to the culture; hence a slave to sin.

— Finally, we are delivered from slavery to the "flesh" — and to sinful humanity — by being incorporated into the flesh of Christ, into the Body of Christ. The law of Christ's Body, the "law of His members" is the Holy Spirit. Hence the full meaning of salvation from sin is to live "*in Christ*," as members of His Body; to live *by* His life, which is grace; and to be ruled and guided and empowered by His Spirit.

The "Body of Christ" means the community of
believers who are united to Christ as Head and
animated by His Spirit. There is in this Body a real
union of each individual member with Christ that is a
mystery: the mystery of grace. ("Grace" just means
"favor," and it is the favor of sharing in the life of
God). To be "in Christ" means to share in Christ's
life — His divine life — just as cells in the human
body live by the life of the whole. So membership in
the Body of Christ is primarily union with Jesus
through that participation in His divine life which we
call "grace." And this union is a mystery, just as grace
is a mystery.

But full membership in Christ also means membership in the *community* of believers who are His
Body on earth. We who came under the domination
of sin through our contact with the human race which
has been infected by sin for centuries are withdrawn
from the power of sin through our contact with
humanity renewed through Christ. What sin, acting in
and through people, has done to us, grace — also
acting in and through people — can undo. As we were
wounded through our contact with sinful humanity,
so we are healed through our contact with redeemed
humanity. Christ heals us, acting not only directly,
through His Spirit poured out in our hearts, but also
through the members of His Body with whom we live
and interact. We are delivered "from this body under
the power of death" (*Romans* 7:24) through our contact with this new Body which is under the power of
life in the Holy Spirit.

When we say, then, that Jesus saves us, we mean
that salvation is an ongoing process. It is not complete until we are completely delivered from the
woundedness of sin within us, and that takes a

lifetime. Jesus is not just the Savior who was; He didn't just save us in one act. He is the Savior who is, who is saving us now through His present action on us. To accept Him as Savior means to enter into a lifelong process of interaction with Him, and with His Body on earth, the Church.

When we say that Jesus "saves us from sin" we mean more than that He pardons us, or wins for us the Father's forgiveness. We mean that He frees us from the accumulated power of sin in the world, and in ourselves, by uniting us to Himself in His saving Body on earth, which is the Church.

If we understand our need to be freed from the power of sin that is at work in us; and if we understand that Jesus — through His Body on earth, through His Spirit sent into our hearts, and through all His continuing, saving activity in our lives right now — continues to be the "saving presence of God on earth," then we will have added another answer to our question, "Why Jesus?":

"He will save His people from their sins."

### CHAPTER THREE: JESUS IS DELIVERANCE FROM SIN — *Matthew* 1:21

*Summary:*

1. Jesus is the "saving presence of God on earth." His saving action on us is not a once-and-for-all act, or even just a series of interventions; it is a constant, enduring action. We are *being* saved through our relationship with Jesus, i.e., through our continuous *interaction* with Him.
2. The "sin" from which Jesus delivers us is not just an act or a series of actions involving personal guilt. We are weakened, blinded and misdirected by that "sin" or sinfulness which is an abiding infection within us. We are wounded and conditioned by our environment. There are within us destructive patterns of emotion, thought and behavior which are in us the fruit of the sin of the world. Jesus delivers us from these.

3. Jesus saves us by incorporating us into Himself — into His own Body. He does this even visibly, by incorporating us into His Church. As members of Christ we receive His Spirit — a new Spirit of light and power to live by. As members of His Body on earth we enter into a new human environment, the community of the redeemed. In the measure that the members of this community act by the Spirit, in union with Jesus their Head, their interaction with one another is healing and redemptive. And so is their witness to the world.

4. To accept salvation in the full Christian sense of the word means to enter into an abiding, active relationship of healing with Jesus Christ through active, participative membership in His Church. Through our interaction with sinful humanity we were enslaved; through our interaction with redeemed humanity we are set free.

*Questions for prayer and discussion:*

1. What destructive patterns of reaction, attitude or behavior can I identify in myself that I have never consciously chosen? Are they in any way the result of the sin of the world? How?

2. How does Jesus offer to save me from these destructive patterns? What is the role of His own humanity (of His words and example) in this saving action? What is the role of His Spirit? Of His Body on earth?

3. What does "salvation" mean? Is it a once-and-for-all act or an ongoing process? Can salvation be more or less complete? How is it going on in me right now? What am I doing to foster it?

4. This chapter invites me to relate to Jesus in His Body on earth as an ongoing, continuing source of salvation. What decision will I make in response to this invitation? Why?

# CHAPTER FOUR

## JESUS IS FULLNESS OF LIFE

Does salvation just mean deliverance from sin? Or, to put the question another way, if sin means to "miss the mark," to "fall short," what is the mark we are enabled to hit when we are saved by Jesus Christ?

The key to the answer is given in the first chapter of Matthew:

> Now this is how the birth of Jesus Christ came about. When his mother Mary was engaged to Joseph, but before they lived together, she was found with child through the power of the Holy Spirit. (*Matthew* 1:18)

Jesus was both God and man. In the body that was conceived in Mary's womb the divine and the human were united. This took place through a double gift of self: God's gift of Himself to Mary, and through her to the human race; Mary's gift of herself to God, which also was a gift to the human race.

And already we have here the pattern of "Salvation." Salvation is going to consist in a union of the divine and the human in one body; in a free and willing gift of God to man and of man to God. And everytime this mutual gift is made, the whole human race will benefit from it.

This means that the "mark" salvation enables us
to hit is not the human mark. It is not the ideal of
perfect human behavior. It is the divine mark: the
level of behavior that is proper to God alone. Jesus
announced this in the first sermon of His that Matthew records, the Sermon on the Mount: "You have
heard the commandment [declaring the human ideal],
'You shall love your countryman but hate your
enemy.' My command to you [declaring the divine
ideal of behavior like that of God Himself] is: love
your enemies, pray for your persecutors."

The old commandments were based on what is
appropriate for human nature. It is a natural thing for
people to love, support and be concerned about their
own family, social group, countrymen. It is also
natural for them to leave those who are thought of as
"the others" — strangers, aliens, people with whom
there is no natural or social bond — to take care of
themselves. This is to "hate" in a neutral sense. One's
enemies, of course, one can hate more actively!

Jesus changes all that. He proposes as man's
standard of living the love that is proper to God
Himself. If we love our enemies, "This will prove that
you are sons of your heavenly Father, for his sun rises
on the bad and the good, he rains on the just and the
unjust." To sum it up: "If you love those who love you
. . . and if you greet your brothers only, what is so
praiseworthy about that? Do not pagans do as much?
In a word, you must be made perfect as your heavenly
Father is perfect" (*Matthew* 5:43-48).

We see from this that when Jesus heals us of the
woundedness of sin, He does not just bring us back to
par. Jesus heals what is deficient in us as human
beings by lifting us beyond the human to the divine.
He shares with us the attitudes and values of God,

and the power to live by them. At the same time, He doesn't leave the human behind. He doesn't take us as persons "out of" our human natures the way one might take the driver out of a car and make him the pilot of an airplane instead. No more than God the Son left His divinity behind when He became man, does He ask us to leave our humanity behind when we become sharers in His divine life.

And so the formula for Christian salvation is the same as the formula for Christ's own reality: "fully human, fully divine." We are called to participate in God's own level of thoughts and desires, of life and activity, as fully as it is possible for a human being to do so, and we are called to become *more* human through this rather than less. The Jesus who lifts us up to share in God's divine life is the same Jesus who as God the Son came down to share in our human life. To be "saved," therefore, means to live the mystery of the divine and the human made one.

This is what Jesus meant when He said, "I came that they might have life, and have it in all of its fullness" (see *John* 10:10). This is what Jesus came for, and this is the meaning of "salvation."

Obviously, then, any denial of human values is a distortion of Christianity. In the measure that we reject anything that is good in human life we reject some measure of salvation.[1] The Christian is not anti-intellectual, opposed to progress, suspicious of pleasure, uptight about sex, afraid of spontaneity, or ashamed to enjoy life. Christians do not believe that the way to become more (authentically) spiritual is to work at being less physical. Even when it is necessary to impose controls on the body and on bodily desires (see 1 *Corinthians* 9:27), the aim of this Christian asceticism is not *suppression* of the physical, but to

make the physical the *expression* of the soul. When
we as persons are so integrated that our bodies and all
our bodily actions are the perfect expression of our
authentic, graced selves, then we can rejoice that
Jesus has made us whole.[2]

All Christians are by definition humanists, therefore, but not mere humanists. There is nothing human
that Christians reject or deny; there is also nothing
human that Christians do not transcend and live on a
higher level by grace. Jesus did not just take to
Himself a human nature; He elevated that nature to
share in the life of God, and everything Jesus did that
was human was also simultaneously divine.

For God to raise our human activity — our
thoughts, desires, choices, decisions — to the level of
His own divine activity, our free cooperation is
required. This does not just mean that we say to God,
"O.K., I accept: please raise everything in me to the
level you desire; act in me and through me as you
will." That would be abdication. We would then be
like robots in whom God speaks and acts as if
through inert matter. God can speak that way in a
burning bush. When he speaks through human beings, however, it has to be in an action that is just as
much ours as His. For God to inflame the world
through us our hearts must be burning within us (see
*Exodus* 3:1 ff. and *Luke* 24:32).

Our union with God in grace is like a partnership. It is a cooperation between two free persons. We
and God act together, both of us freely, and according
to our natures, to produce one single act. God doesn't
push us aside like incompetent children and do "His
thing" within us. And we of ourselves are not capable
of doing anything at all on the divine level of grace
(see *John* 15:4-5). But in the measure that we

surrender ourselves to God's action within us — to the inspirations and movements of His Holy Spirit dwelling in our hearts — and are willing to cooperate with Him, then we and God can act together in a way that unites all that both of us are in one single action.

And this kind of action, our graced activity that is the result of God's free gift of self to us and of our free gift of self to Him, is always a saving action. It furthers our own redemption and that of all mankind.

If, for any reason, our human natures cannot cooperate on the level that is required of them, God will simply wait. This explains, for example, why it took Christians more than eighteen hundred years to abolish slavery, and another hundred years after that to see that segregation was wrong. People were just not prepared culturally to think the thoughts that would bring into concrete human expression what God was saying in their hearts (and had been saying since the dawn of Christianity): "Love one another as I have loved you." Christians were able to repeat God's words, and sincerely love them in their abstractness, or in their application to decisions they were prepared for. But the great mass of Christian society was humanly incapable — that is, intellectually, emotionally and culturally incapable — of making the obvious application of these words to their concrete situation. They could not utter their *own* creative word of knowledge, breathing in God's word, "Love," and breathing out — with Him — that same word "made flesh" in the concrete circumstances of their own time and place: "Love your slaves and free them; love other races as God loves you: be *one* with them!"

For an action to be human it must be concrete. It must take place in time and space. And for any truth that deals with living to be humanly possessed it must be seen and spoken creatively in the actual, human world of one's own time, place and culture. Until we are able to *re-utter* Jesus' words in a way that relates them creatively to our own human situation, we have not really interiorized Christ's words, have not made them our own — and we cannot speak His truth prophetically in our own time.

Jesus the Head does not act incarnately in the world without the free and personal cooperation of His Body. Jesus will not — *cannot*, without changing the meaning of salvation — speak out or act through His Body on earth until His members are humanly able to understand and see for themselves what He wants to say in them and humanly willing to accept it, embrace it, and adopt it as their own choice and desire. Jesus takes partnership seriously. He has not called us to be servants or slaves who just take orders without knowing what their master is about, but friends (see *John* 15:15). When we act with Jesus by grace we must act as partners. This means that we ourselves must understand with Him, choose with Him, and decide.[3]

For God to enlighten our minds through faith, for example, He normally requires that we have some human knowledge of the truth He is communicating directly to our hearts. I say "normally requires," because God's gift of self is not limited: He can communicate His life, His Spirit, His light and love to tiny infants and to retarded children whose minds are not capable of expressing God's truth in words (see *Luke* 1:44). But as grace appears in the ordinary adult, and when it comes to Christ's *expression* of Himself in and through people, His self-expression is limited to what their human natures are capable of.

St. Paul recognized this blending of grace with nature when he wrote: "How can they believe unless they have heard of him? And how can they hear unless there is someone to preach? . . . Faith, then, comes through hearing, and what is heard is the word of Christ" (*Romans* 10:14-17).

Paul might have gone on to add, continuing the same line of reasoning, "How can they grow, through faith, in understanding of what they hear unless they *think*? Understanding comes through reflection, and what is reflected on is the truth we know through faith."

God doesn't by-pass our human way of learning and just infuse His attitudes and values into our heads, the way someone might write words on a piece of blank paper or record a message on a tape. He takes us more seriously than that. Whatever we know and understand through faith, and appreciate through the divine gift of wisdom and love, we have to come to understand and love humanly as well. Otherwise it isn't really ours. And this means we usually have to work at it — at least as much as we work at understanding and appreciating any other truth or value. If this were not so, if our human powers could just remain inert and passive while God infused His own attitudes and values into our heads, then our human natures would count for nothing. It would not be ourselves, the human beings that we are, who would be acting divinely, but simply God acting in us without any involvement of our natural equipment.

Normally speaking, then, there is no growth in grace which is not accompanied by human growth as well. We grow in the human knowledge of God's word and in graced, supernatural understanding of it simultaneously.[4]

Everyone grows at a different pace; and the whole Body of Christ, or any particular Christian community, grows more slowly than its most fervent members. And so Jesus keeps His Body growing in wisdom, grace and love by speaking out through the "prophets" — through those individuals who are thinking and praying over His words and are able to hear and express humanly what the Spirit is saying in their hearts. If any community or group is prepared to listen to the prophets, to reflect on and respond to what they say, then Jesus can move them also to cooperate with Him in what He is trying to do on earth.[5]

Our partnership with Jesus is, in a sense, both good news and bad news. It is good news because God takes our humanity seriously. He does not brush it aside but uses it, develops it and transforms it.

The bad news, however, or what might appear to us to be bad news, is this: because Jesus has made us His partners, and not just His slaves or uncomprehending servants, He cannot act on earth now as freely as He could when the only body He had was the one He was born with. That body — His own human nature — was perfectly united to His person, perfectly subordinated to His divinity. And therefore Jesus was able through His own human nature to give perfect expression to all that he wanted to say or to do. Even here there were limitations, of course: if God in Jesus had thought or spoken in ways that were completely incompatible with His background, culture and education as a first-century Jew, God would not have been acting in Jesus as truly one with His human nature. Jesus knew nothing, for example, about nuclear physics and could not have made any statement about the morality of the atom bomb. This kind of limitation follows from the very fact that God is acting through a human nature. But there is one limitation God was not subject to in Jesus. The human nature of Jesus was not in any way under the domination of sin. No sin, either His own (for He was sinless) or the sins of the world (although He bore them) could in any way prevent, impede or distort the self-expression of God which Jesus gave through His own humanity and human actions. Sin had no power over Him at all.

But sin does have some power still over us who are Christ's Body now. It is true that in the measure we surrender to Christ our Head and let Him rule in us, in that same measure we are delivered from the domination of sin (see *Romans* 6:12-14). But while the process of our own subordination to Christ is still incomplete, during the period when Jesus is still purifying His Body, the Church, and preparing her for total union with Himself (see *Ephesians* 5:22-32), Christ is not able to speak and act in us with total freedom. We have grace, which means we enjoy the favor of union with Him, but we are not "full of grace," which would mean we are so united to Him that our human natures no longer block Him at all. Or, to put this in other words, we are "saved," because we are united with Him; but our salvation is not complete, because our union with Him is not yet total.

"Salvation," then, is a divine and human reality. It consists essentially in our union with Christ as members of His Body. But it is not complete until our union with Christ is complete, until our surrender to Him is total. As long as the salvation of each individual member is not complete, there is a sense in which Jesus Himself — Jesus Head and members —

has not yet come to completion. The "whole Christ,"
that "one new man" (*Ephesians* 2:15) who is the goal
of all creation (*Ephesians* 1:10; *Colossians* 1:15-20)
does not grow just in numbers, by the addition of new
members; He also grows to perfection as the members
become more and more conformed to the Head
through faith, through hope and through love. Bringing the Body of Christ to perfection in this way is the
"work of salvation" that continues to the end of time,
and all of us are called to participate in it:

> It is he who gave apostles, prophets, evangelists,
> pastors and teachers in roles of service for the faithful
> to build up the body of Christ, till we become one in
> faith and in the knowledge of God's Son, and form
> that perfect man who is Christ come to full stature.
> (*Ephesians* 4:11-13)

If we ask ourselves again, "Why Jesus?" the
answer comes: "Because in Jesus my humanity itself
is saved." Through the salvation He gives — that is,
through grace, or the favor of sharing in His life as
members of His Body — nothing that we are is
destroyed, thrown aside, or rejected. In our union
with Him we remain integral human beings, not only
allowed but required to act with all of our human
powers of intellect and will.

But through union with Christ the use we make
of our human powers is lifted to a higher level: in our
human acts of thinking, choosing, understanding, and
deciding, we participate as partners in Christ's own
divine act of knowing, loving and willing. We see and
understand "in Christ," as members of His Body
sharing in His divine vision of truth. He sees and
understands in us, as Head of His Body, acting in the
concrete, human reality of each member according to
the circumstances of each one's time, place and

culture. In the American, Jesus sees things from an American point of view; in the Japanese He sees things from a Japanese point of view; and in Him both points of view are reconciled. In a woman all that Jesus thinks and says and does is characterized by her femininity; in a man by his masculinity. In His Body on earth Jesus sees and acts simultaneously as young and old, healthy and sick, liberal and conservative, black and white, western and oriental, and in Him all things are made one, brought into harmony and unity without losing their distinctive identity. He gives Himself to us without destroying what we are. We give ourselves to Him and come to share in all He is without ceasing to be what we are.

This is what salvation is: the union of the human and the divine in Jesus Christ, and in us who are the members of His redeemed Body on earth. This salvation is another answer to our questions.

"Why Jesus?"

"Because in Him we are called to be fully human and fully divine."

---

### FOOTNOTES

[1]This is not an argument against Christian renunciation. Authentic Christian renunciation is never the renunciation — much less the rejection — of any value as such. It may, however, be the renunciation of the normal human *means* to a certain value in order to attain that same value on a higher, transcedent level. See my book *Cloud By Day — Fire By Night*, Vol. I, ch. 12 (Dimension Books, 1980).

[2]See the application of this idea to sexual expression in my book *The Good News About Sex*, ch. 23: "Wholeness as an Ideal" (St. Anthony Messenger Press, 1979).

[3]This is not to deny that there are moments when we must follow Christ in darkness, in pure faith, pure trust, without understanding why He is dealing with us as He is. That is true of any deep friendship, human as well as divine. But we on our part must try as much as possible, to come to a human understanding of all

Jesus said and did. This is a human understanding enlightened by faith and grace, of course.

[4]The graced understanding, at least, requires some proportionate human understanding — which does not have to be academic knowledge. But human knowledge of God's word does not automatically carry with it graced understanding. There are such things as spiritual eggheads too!

[5]We have an example of this in John Woolman and in his fellow Quakers who, long before the American Revolution, paid attention to Woolman when he began to argue that slavery was incompatible with the following of Christ. It took Woolman fourteen years to convince his fellow Quakers, but in 1776, four years after his death, the Quakers of Pennsylvania voted to free all their slaves. They were prophetically in advance of their times because they were able to listen to Christ. See *The Journal of John Woolman*, ed. Janet Whitney (Regnery, 1950) and my book *His Way*, ch. 9: "The Salt in the Shakers" (St. Anthony Messenger Press, 1977).

## CHAPTER FOUR: JESUS IS FULLNESS OF LIFE —
*Matthew* 1:18-25

*Summary:*

1. The name "Jesus" means "God saves." To "save" human life means to preserve it, to repair or heal it, to bring it to fullness and perfection. This is what Jesus came to do.

2. Jesus does this by taking us *beyond* the level of human life and behavior to share in the fullness of God's own light and life; in the fullness, that is, of God's own knowledge of Himself; of His own attitudes, values, power to love and to enjoy. Our human nature is saved by being brought beyond "self-actualization" to the actualization of all its capacity by grace (i.e., by the favor of union with God).

3. Christianity as a religion calls us to be "fully human and fully divine." Christians accept and value everything that is authentically human, just as Jesus did. At the same time, Christians aim at living all human values on a divine level as children of the Father and "sons in the Son." God's own level of knowing and loving is the level proper to us as born again in Christ.

4. In raising us to the level of divine life, God does not leave our human natures behind. Our human development and our growth in grace go together; they mutually depend on each other and complement each other.

*Questions for prayer and discussion:*

1. What level of ideals do I aim at in by behavior: At what is *good* (as opposed to evil)? At what bears *witness* to Christ (as opposed to what is just acceptable)? At what is like God Himself?
2. How do I experience my actions as being both human and divine? Is there any human value I reject or shy away from? Can I identify ways I go beyond the human to act on a level that belongs to God alone?
3. How have I experienced that my growth in grace (i.e., in understanding of the faith, in acceptance of Christ's ideals, in ability to live by them) keeps pace with and depends on my human development? What can I identify in the development of the Church which shows this same interdependence of the divine and the human?" How does this interdependence "save" our humanity?
4. This chapter invites me to live through Jesus Christ on a level that is "fully human and fully divine." What concrete decision can I make that is a response to this invitation?

## CHAPTER FIVE

## JESUS IS GOD HUMANLY CLOSE

We have seen something of *what* salvation is: Jesus delivers us from our deepest loneliness and offers us intimate friendship with God; He saves our lives from meaninglessness by calling us to share in His own work and mission; He delivers us from the power of sin in ourselves and in the world; and He calls us to live the fullness of human and divine life made one in Him: "I came that they might have life, and have it to the full" (*John* 10:10).

The next thing Matthew invites us to look at is *how* Jesus does this. He does it by being *Emmanuel*: "God-with-us."

We have already seen how in the Scriptures a person's name is understood to express the inmost reality of the person. This might be his nature, as when God revealed His name — "I AM" — to Moses (*Exodus* 3: 11-15); or it might be his special call or mission, as when God changed Abram's name to Abraham (*Genesis* 17:5). A name can also express relationship (see *Hosea* 1:6,9; 2:1-3). The name *Emmanuel* expresses all three of these: Jesus is "God-with-us" by *nature*, since He is God made man; He came, and was *sent* by the Father precisely to be

God-with-us, the saving presence of God in our midst;
and His *relationship* with us is one of closeness,
presence, the mediation of God to men.

Jesus is Mediator by nature. This is His mission,
and this is His fundamental relationship with us. He is
the one in whom and through whom we see God,
experience God, come into life-giving contact with
God (see *John* 14:6-10). He is *Emmanuel* — "God-
with-us." In and through Jesus God gives Himself to
us in concrete, human ways. And because of God's
human presence in Jesus we are able to respond to
Him, to interact with Him, in human ways of our
own.

We may agree that this was true when Jesus
walked the earth in His own body. But how is it still
true today? Is Jesus still "Emmanuel" for us as
completely and truly as He was for His apostles and
for those who heard and touched and followed Him
in Galilee? Or did the Incarnation, for all practical
purposes, end when Jesus ascended into heaven?

This is a fundamental question for us to ask,
because the answer we give will determine our whole
approach to God and to the spiritual life. Does Jesus
still speak to us in human words? Act on us through
human touches and gestures? Reveal Himself to us in
human form? And can we affect His reality as a
person by our own human words and actions? Can we
really interact with *Him*, now that He has ascended
into heaven, and do anything for *Him*? Or must we be
content with just helping other people, knowing that
it pleases Christ and that He counts our kindness as if
it were done to Himself? (see *Matthew* 10:40-42).

When we ask ourselves, "Why Jesus?" can we
answer, "Because He is *here now* for me to interact
with; because in Jesus God is present to me now in

human form"? And if so, what do we mean by this?

The first thing we mean is that Jesus speaks to us now in human words.

This speaking is just as real, and just as human as the conversations we have with our friends. It isn't as *facile* — that is, it isn't something so automatic and effortless for us that we can engage in it all day long without even thinking, the way we sometimes babble on to other people. Words are cheap to us, precisely because they come so easily. A lot of times we talk just to be talking, without really saying anything. And since we know that others do the same, we frequently don't even bother to listen. Much of our speech isn't real human communication at all, because our persons are not being expressed in our words.

The same is true of writing. It used to be that writing was very rare — so rare that it was considered sacred. Then people were very careful about what they wrote. They composed the way artists paint, with attention to every detail. And people read with the same attention and respect, knowing that every word had been chosen with care by a person trying to express something very deep and important to his soul.

But as it became easier and easier, and cheaper and cheaper to multiply written words — through printing, mimeographing, xeroxing, computer printouts, etc. — people began to pay less and less attention both to what they read and to what they wrote. Speedreading and scanning became indispensable tools for anyone whose job requires keeping up with what is being said. This is because so much communication is three parts clutter to one part content and style.

But there is no speedreading the Bible. And when
we talk to Jesus, or He to us, it is pure communication of person to person. Jesus doesn't just rattle on,
and He warns us not to: "In your prayer do not rattle
on like the pagans. They think they will win a hearing
by the sheer multiplication of words. Do not imitate
them" (*Matthew* 6:7-8). When we communicate with
God in prayer we do it the way we should communicate with other human beings: by speaking and listening to words which on both sides come from the heart
and express one's deepest person, mind and desire.
And this is the kind of speaking with God in human
words that Jesus has made possible.

He made it possible by expressing His own heart
and soul in human words to us. They are written in
the Scriptures. When we read them, however, it is not
like reading any other book. The author of the
Scriptures is neither absent nor dead as we read. He is
there, and He Himself is speaking directly to our
hearts as we read His written words. This makes the
Scriptures unique as a book: they are the only book
we can read through which the living person of the
author is expressing Himself to us person-to-person,
right then and there, through his written words, just
as a person expresses himself to another through his
living voice in conversation.

When we make an effort to communicate with
Jesus through the Scriptures, taking His words seriously, asking ourselves what they mean, trying to take
a stance toward their content with our wills and our
hearts, this is a divine-human conversation.[1]

It is a human conversation because the medium
of communication is human words. Jesus is communicating with us the way human beings communicate
with each other: by expressing His thoughts and

desires in human speech. It is also a divine conversation, because the person of Jesus is actively involved
in expressing Himself to us at that moment. And in
order that we might understand His mind, which is
beyond all human understanding, He is enlightening
us from within by the gift of His Holy Spirit. The
same truth that Jesus is speaking to us humanly
through the words of the Scriptures, the Holy Spirit is
speaking simultaneously in our hearts, making it
intelligible to us through the light of His own divine
knowledge which, when we share in it, is called the
"light of faith."

Jesus has said and will say to us through the
Scriptures everything we need to hear in order to
know Him intimately as a person. Sometimes people
say, "I don't believe I can get to know Jesus through
the words that He speaks in the Scriptures, but if I
could just talk to Him myself for awhile, and ask Him
the questions I want to ask, then I think I could know
Him."

What questions would you ask?

Suppose you came home one evening and found
Jesus sitting on your bed. Suppose He said, "Ask me
any question about myself you'd like to ask — but
just about myself. Don't ask me when the end of the
world is coming or how to make a profit in your
business, or even what I want *you* to do to please me.
Leave all those questions aside for now and just ask
me about myself. What do you want to know about
my own personal thoughts, feelings, desires?"

What would you ask?

I've tried this out with different groups of people.
After a few false starts, in which people are asking
questions that seem to be about Jesus but really are
about themselves or their own problems (such as

"Jesus, what do you think about war? Should I let myself be drafted?") we discovered that for almost every question people asked, we already knew the answer from the Scriptures.

"Lord, what kind of people do you like?" — and we thought of the people He chose to be His apostles (*Matthew* 4:18 ff. and 9:9 ff.); His praise of John the Baptizer (*Matthew* 11:7 ff); His admiration of the widow who gave her last two copper coins away (*Luke* 21:1 ff.); the people he felt comfortable with and who felt comfortable with Him (*Matthew* 9:10 ff.; 15:30 ff.; *Luke* 18:15 ff); the wealthy little man He chose to have dinner with (*Luke* 19:1 ff.). And these examples are just a beginning.

"Lord, what kind of things make you sad?" Then we remembered how He cried over the death of His friend Lazarus (*John* 11:35); and wept over Jerusalem (*Luke* 19:41) and was filled with sadness at the approach of His own passion and death (*Mark* 14:34).

These questions are only a sample, of course, but they give some concrete idea of how the questions we have about the personality of Jesus are already answered in the Scriptures. We only have to look to find them. Jesus still communicates with us humanly through His words.

Another way Jesus deals with us humanly today is through the sacramental ministry of the Church.

Jesus was a great toucher. In the Gospels we find Him laying hands on the sick (*Mark* 6:4; *Luke* 4:40), touching the eyes of the blind (*Matthew* 20:34), taking a little girl by the hand (*Matthew* 9:25), letting Mary of Magdala wash His feet with her tears and dry them with her hair (*Luke* 7:38) and taking it for granted that a father would embrace his son (*Luke* 15:20). He made use of physical things, not only in His preaching and storytelling, but in His own communication with people. He expresses Himself through oil and water, bread and wine, mud paste, salt and little children! His greatest act of self-expression was through wood and flesh and blood.[2]

The essence of sacramental ministry, or of that grace (i.e., favor) of increased union with God which we call "sacramental grace," lies in the fact that the grace of the sacraments comes to us through some human, physical contact with Jesus acting in His Body on earth today. When Jesus gives us new life by pouring water and speaking humanly the words of baptism, we have been sacramentally baptized. Other people receive "baptism of desire" (see *Matthew* 2:1-12: the pagan astrologers) or "baptism of blood" (see *Matthew* 2:16-18: the Jewish babies massacred in hatred of Jesus: Christian tradition has accepted the Magi as saints and the babies as martyrs although none of them ever really knew Jesus or was baptized formally in His name). All three baptisms — water, desire and blood — are sufficient to give us the saving grace of God, to make us reborn children of the Father and heirs of heaven. And since the only way we can live by the divine life of God (grace) is to live as members of Jesus who alone has that divine life, the first effect of baptism — whether of water, blood or desire — is to make us members of Christ's Body on earth. This is the only way we can become children of God. There is only *one* true Son of God: Jesus. He is the "only-begotten Son," and the rest of us are "sons in the Son," true sons of the Father by reason of our incorporation into the Body of Christ His Son. Thus no one is "saved," lifted up to participation in God's eternal life, except through incorporation into the humanity of Jesus. And this is what it means when we say that Jesus, and Jesus alone, is the Mediator between God and man: there is no union with God except through union with Him who is both God and man by nature.

The first effect of any baptism is to make us members of Christ's Body, therefore, because this is what it means to receive "grace" (the favor of union with God). But without sacramental baptism a human contact with Jesus acting in His members, His Body on earth, is missing — both in the act of baptism itself and in the relationship with Jesus that follows after it.

Those who have "baptism of desire," the non-Christians who have been reborn by grace received without explicit knowledge of Jesus, are like members of a body without any contact or coordination with the other members. They live by the life of the body, but cannot participate fully in its action. The channels of communication are not open.

Those who are members of Christ's Body in the full sense, however; that is, those who are also members of the organized community we call the Church, are in constant human interaction with Jesus who lives and acts in His members. In some members Jesus teaches; in others He goes out in generosity to the poor; in others He exercises authority within the community. But in all the members it is Jesus who acts, and acts both divinely and humanly at once:

> Just as each of us has one body with many members, and not all the members have the same function, so we, though many, are one body in Christ and individually members one of another. We have gifts that differ according to the favor bestowed on each of us. One's gift may be prophecy; its use should be in proportion to his faith. It may be the gift of ministry; it should be used for service. One who is a teacher should use his gift for teaching; one with the power of

exhortation should exhort. He who gives alms should do so generously; he who rules should exercise his authority with care; he who performs works of mercy should do so cheerfully. (*Romans* 12:4-8)

Because Jesus acts visibly and tangibly in His Church through His physical, human members, the Church herself can be called the "sacrament of all sacraments," or that one "visible sign instituted by Christ to give grace" which includes all the other sacraments. In the Church we grow in grace through interaction with Jesus in visible, human ways.

In the Church Jesus teaches with a human voice, as once He did in Galilee. He encourages and exhorts; He guides and governs and rules like a shepherd in the midst of his sheep. In the Church Jesus has a healing ministry, both through the words that He speaks in forgiveness of sins and through every ministry and expression of love which restores hope, confidence and joy. In and through the Church Jesus continues to call people to Himself by name, to commission them and send them in His service. In the Church Jesus Himself joins the hands of bride and groom and blesses their gift of self to one another — and through each other to Himself and to the rest of mankind. In the Church Jesus continues to break bread and give it to us saying, "take this, all of you, and eat of it. This is my body, which is given up for you."

In the Church Jesus still touches with the laying on of hands. He still pours water, anoints with oil, gives salt to taste, bread and wine to partake of together. He still speaks with a human voice, ministers in human form through living men and women, and extends His presence to every place where people live and work and act. He is *Emmanuel* — "God-with-us."

Besides His presence through *word* and through *sacrament* — that is, through the Scriptures and through all the sacramental roles and ministries of His Church — Jesus is Emmanuel, "God-with-us" in another way. He is present to us through every charismatic *manifestation of His Spirit* in His human members.

St. Paul teaches that "to each person the manifestation of the Spirit is given for the common good":

> To one the Spirit gives wisdom in discourse, to another the power to express knowledge. Through the Spirit one receives faith; by the same Spirit another is given the gift of healing and still another miraculous powers. Prophecy is given to one; to another power to distinguish one spirit from another. One receives the gift of tongues, another that of interpreting the tongues. But it is one and the same Spirit who produces all these gifts, distributing them to each as he wills. (1 *Corinthians* 12:4-11)

And it is one and the same Jesus who reveals, manifests and expresses Himself through each member who gives external expression to the movement of the Spirit within him.

St. Paul's list of charisms is not meant to be exhaustive, as if every manifestation of the Spirit could be catalogued. He speaks indistinctly of "gifts," "ministries" and "roles of service" in a loose and unsystematic way, even when at times he arranges them in some order of priority or value (see 1 *Corinthians* 12:27-31). There are some functions in the Church which are essential to her integral operation: they must be present, always and everywhere, for the Church to perform her mission as they should. We call these functions sacramental. To initiate and receive new members into the Church, for example, by baptism; to receive back through reconciliation those who have left the Church by apostasy or by sins incompatible with the faith Christians profess; to nourish the members with the word and the Eucharist — for these and other functions clear, distinct empowerment to act in the name of Jesus is required. And for each of these a sacrament exists.

But there are other functions in the Body which are not always required, or not in the same manner at all times and by every local community of believers. These functions are such that when they are taking place it is not essential that in every case everyone should know exactly whether or not it really is Jesus who is speaking or acting in His members. A reasonably accurate discernment is enough. And these are what we call the charismatic gifts. St. Paul gives us a vivid description of the appearance of these charisms during the early Church's celebration of the Eucharist:

> When you assemble, one has a psalm, another some instruction to give, still another a revelation to share; one speaks in a tongue, another interprets. . . . Let no more than two or three prophets speak, and let the rest judge the worth of what they say. (1 *Corinthians* 14:26-29)

It isn't really essential to know whether Jesus is inspiring each particular member who suggests a hymn or offers an insight into the meaning of the Scriptures or its application to concrete, daily living. It is important that the community weigh and try to discern what God is saying through the various members — "let the rest judge the worth of what the prophets say" — but it is not essential that this judgment should always be exact. The charismatic gifts are meant to increase faith and devotion, and when their overall effect is good, it can be presumed they are authentic. If through the manifestation of the Spirit in one another, the members of the Church grow in awareness of the presence and power and love of Jesus Christ in their midst, then these gifts are bearing their fruit, they are another way in which we experience *Emmanuel*, the human presence of Jesus among us.

Finally, because Jesus really is present in His members, because they are truly His Body, we can serve Jesus Himself, and affect the reality of Jesus Himself when we serve and have an effect on His members.

We think immediately of the Last Judgment scene which is built around the repeated statement, "As often as you did it for one of my least brothers, you did it for me. . . . As often as you neglected to do it to one of these least ones, you neglected to do it to me" (see *Matthew* 25:31-46). In this scene people are not rewarded for helping other people in a way that is pleasing to Christ; they are rewarded for serving Jesus Himself in His members.

This is not really difficult to understand; it is just difficult to believe, so we tend not to take it literally. In the back of our minds we tend to assume that this passage in Matthew is just Jesus' poetic way of saying that whatever we do for any human being in need He *takes as if* it were done for Himself and rewards it accordingly. But Jesus is not the head of a company asking us to treat his representatives as if they were Himself; He is the Head of His Body telling us that what we do for the members of His Body is actually done to Himself. What He is saying is not difficult to understand. *How* it can be — how individual, distinct human beings can actually *be* the Body of Christ — is difficult to understand; it is a mystery beyond comprehension, being the mystery of grace itself. But Jesus does not require us to understand how it can be — just to believe that it *is*.

This means that what we want to do for Jesus we can still do for Him — directly and immediately — in other people.[3] He is still *Emmanuel* — God-with-us — for us to love and serve in physical, human ways.[4]

The God who has "drawn near" in Jesus is not just a God we adore and receive from. He is a God who has physical, human needs, needs that we can satisfy. He still asks us for water as He asked the woman at the well in Samaria (*John* 4:7). He continues to ask us for emotional support in His fear and distress, just as He did in His agony in the garden (see *Luke* 14:34). We can laugh with Him, cry with Him, celebrate with Him and comfort Him still because He is humanly present and asking all this of us in His Body on earth today. He not only gives and expresses Himself to us humanly: we can also give and express our love to Him humanly because He is present to receive it. He is *Emmanuel.*

Why Jesus? Because He is a God we can interact with. Through Jesus we can have a human relationship with God. We can interact with Him in a human way. We can reflect on His words and get to know Him. We can form our own personalities in response to His attitudes, values and example. We can experience Him responding to us in the sacraments and taking initiatives in our lives: leading us, inviting us, sending us. We can work for Him, serve Him and be served by Him — just like the people of His own day. He lives and acts and speaks among us still in His Body on earth. He is *Emmanuel.*

## FOOTNOTES

[1] An explanation of *how* to pray over God's words in Scripture is given in chapters three and four of my book *His Way* (St. Anthony Messenger Press, 1977).

[2] For examples see *Mark* 6:13, *Luke* 7:46 (oil); *Matthew* 28:19, *John* 4:7-10 and 13:5 (water); *Matthew* 26:26 ff. (bread and wine); *John* 9:7 (mud paste); *Matthew* 5:13 (salt) and *Matthew* 18:2 (little children).

[3] To be precise, what we are saying here does not apply to the service we render to every human being. It is only true of what we do for the actual members of Christ's Body, because these are the only people who actually *are* Christ in the way we have been describing. To say indiscriminately that whatever is done to any human being on earth is done to Christ is to strip the statement of any Scriptural or theological content. This reduces it to a vague affirmation of the "universal brotherhood of all men," which is based on nothing more than membership in the human race as such. The brotherhood Christians believe in is that which belongs to all who are children (not just creatures) of God through rebirth as members of the Body of Christ: those who through baptism have *become* "sons in the Son."

For *practical* purposes, however, which is what we are mainly concerned with, and which the judgment scene in Matthew is also concerned with, we have to treat *all* men and women as our brothers and sisters in Christ. This is for two reasons: first, all are *called* to be one with us in this relationship through grace; and secondly, we have no way of knowing that this or that particular individual is *not* already reborn by grace as a member of Christ. A person may not know the name of Jesus or belong to any church, and still be a Christian through an unrecognized "baptism of desire." Hence when we insist on the truth that these words of Matthew apply only to those who are actual members of Christ's Body, this should not affect our *conduct* toward others in any way; it should just keep us aware of how literally Jesus means it when He says, "as long as you did it to one of these, you did it to me." Jesus is saying something here which only became possible through His Incarnation and our incorporation into His Body through grace.

[4] See my book *The Good News About Sex*, chapter 15: "The Dimension Jesus Added: The Mystery Of Sacramental Sex," for the way this doctrine applies to the gift of self that married people make to one another in marriage and in the physical expression of love in intercourse. Because of the sacrament of matrimony, both partners in the marriage are giving themselves to Christ in each

other, and Christ is giving Himself in and through the gift that each one makes to the other.

## CHAPTER FIVE: JESUS IS GOD HUMANLY CLOSE — *Matthew* 1:23

*Summary:*

1. Jesus saves by being *Emmanuel* — "God-with-us." In Jesus the light and power of God are revealed to us through Christ's human actions. As God-man His nature and mission is to be *Mediator*, the "bridge" through which we can have true, personal, human relationship with God.
2. Jesus is human. He speaks to us in human words, reveals His personality to us in human actions. He teaches, forgives, heals and encourages us by human gestures. By coming to know Jesus the way we come to know other human beings, we can have authentic human friendship with God.
3. Jesus continues to reveal Himself to us today through His words and actions expressed to us in Scripture; through His Spirit speaking in our hearts; through His real presence and activity in His Body on earth, the Church. In all ages Jesus saves by being "God-with-us" — by acting on us humanly, both through His own humanity and the human natures of those joined to Him by grace. The Incarnation is forever.
4. The decision to be a Christian is precisely the decision to base one's life on interaction with God speaking and giving Himself to us humanly in Jesus Christ.

*Questions for prayer and discussion:*

1. What part does the humanity of Jesus play in my life now? How do I deal with His human words, His human example? Do I let Him express Himself in my humanity? How?
2. Have I ever tried to get to know Jesus — His mind, His heart, His personality — through reflecting on His words and example in Scripture the way I would reflect on any other person's words and behavior? Is this something I choose to do now? Why?
3. What has been my experience of Jesus acting on me humanly through the Church? Through the sacraments? Through the members of His Body on earth? Do I recognize these actions as the actions of Jesus Himself?
4. This chapter invites me to build my whole life — my personality, my goals, my development — on this interaction with God speaking humanly in Jesus. Am I decided to do this? Why?

## CHAPTER SIX

## JESUS IS AN INESCAPABLE QUESTION

Why Jesus? Why should we bother to decide what our stance toward Him will be?

Matthew's next answer is: "Because it is impossible not to." Jesus is the universal Lord and destiny of the human race — of every man and woman born into this world. No one can escape confronting His reality because He is in fact the Lord and destiny of all, and He reveals Himself to all without exception. All were made for Him (see *Colossians* 1:15-20; *Ephesians* 1:3-23). All were made through Him. He is the light of the world and the life of the world. Every human being was created to receive eternal life through the knowledge of Jesus Christ (see *John* 17:3).

Through him all things came into being,
and apart from him nothing came to be.
Whatever came to be in him, found life,
life for the light of men. (*John* 1:3-4)

Matthew's way of saying this is through a story. After telling us about the angel's visit to Joseph he takes us in imagination to the other end of the world. He tells us that after Jesus was born in Bethlehem some pagan astrologers — wise men, "magi" — from a faraway eastern land arrived in Jerusalem inquiring,

"Where is the newborn king of the Jews? We observed his star at its rising and have come to pay him homage" (*Matthew* 2:1-2).

Even these pagan astrologers, who lived somewhere in the distant vagueness of "the east," men who had no communication with Israel or acquaintance with her traditions, even they were confronted by the event of Christ's birth and summoned to respond. This is the point of Matthew's story.

And the point addresses us all. No man or woman born into this world can fail, at some time or another, in some manner or another, to encounter Jesus Christ. He is the light which sooner or later pierces through the darkness and penetrates to the heart of every human person (*John* 1:9).

The story of the astrologers shows us how God addresses every human being in the language he or she is best prepared to understand. The magi were not Jews but pagans. As astrologers they sought knowledge of God through the stars. And so God spoke to them through a star. He addressed them through the symbols of their own religion — their pagan religion. But even while He called them through a star He was calling them to worship, not the stars, but Jesus Christ.

In the response of the magi we have all the characteristics of authentic "baptism of desire." But these same characteristics are the ingredients of every authentic act of *faith*. Therefore they are of personal interest to us. They show us what our own — what every authentic — response of faith to Jesus Christ must be.

First, the magi were *called and inspired by God*. The initiative in their movement came from God; it was a work of grace. The astrologers did not "discover" Jesus or God through their religion, or by their own human efforts at all. They were invited. God came to them, addressing them, summoning them, calling them to His Son through a star accompanied by an interior movement of grace.

Secondly, their response was *open-ended and unconditional.* They were not responding to the star, or to anything limited and finite. They were responding to Whoever it was, Whatever it was, who was inviting them and calling them through the star. This made their response as unlimited, as infinite, as the Person to whom they were responding.

Had the astrologers known about Abraham they would have recognized that God was requiring of them the same act of faith He demanded of him: "The LORD said to Abram [who, like the astrologers, was still a pagan at the time], 'Go forth from the land of your kinsfolk and from your father's house to a land that I will show you'" (*Genesis* 12:1). Abraham didn't know where he was going either, or how far. Like the astrologers, he was responding, not primarily to a message that he heard, but to a Person he could not see. And this is characteristic of every authentic act of faith. We ask God where He is leading us, and the answer is always, "To Me" (see *John* 1:37-39).

A third characteristic of the astrologers' response (and of every authentic act of faith) is that it was, in fact, the acceptance of *something definite,* even though they didn't know what that was.

We have just seen that faith must be open-ended. For an act of faith to be truly *divine* — that is, graced, supernatural, having God Himself as its object — it must go beyond everything finite and limited and be a response to the Person of God Himself. But at the same time, for an act of faith to be a truly *human*

act — for it to have reality and substance here on
earth — it must be an acceptance of something definite, something concrete and specific. To respond to
generalities is not to respond at all.

The astrologers are an example of this. They
were not following a star across the desert out of
devotion to abstract truth. They were committed
from the moment they set out to accepting the
concrete, specific truth of Jesus Christ and of His
Gospel, whatever that might be and however it might
be revealed to them. And this was before they even
knew the name of Jesus. When they arrived at
Herod's court they did not say, "We seek enlightment;
whatever is true and good we will reverence." They
were much more definite than that. "Where is the
newborn king of the Jews? We have come to worship
him."

The astrologers accepted in advance the concrete
reality and message of Jesus — before they had even
seen Him, before they had heard one word of His
revelation. Their act of faith was given to God
speaking in the concrete, in the specific words and
teaching of Jesus — it was faith in His Incarnation —
even though they did not know what this specific
reality would be. "We have come to worship *him*."
They believed already in whatever concrete reality
their star was leading them to. And it was Jesus.

An act of faith, to be real, has to be a definite
human act. Just to affirm and accept the intellect's
natural orientation toward truth in general is not to
make a response to God revealing Himself. And so
the astrologers' "baptism of desire" was not just a
conscious, sincere openness to all truth; it was a
specific response to a movement from God inviting
them to the concrete revelation made in Jesus Christ.

"Where is the newborn king of the Jews? We have come to worship *him*."

What this tells us is that every human being is called in some way by God, through some symbol or sign recognizable to each, to accept the concrete reality and revelation of Jesus Christ. Some people may never actually learn, during this life, what they were responding to when they accepted to follow their star. They may never encounter Jesus by name, hear His revelation in human words or learn what it is He teaches. Still they are Christians if they have already accepted in advance to worship the concrete reality to which God is calling them through their star, because that reality is Jesus. If the astrologers had died in the desert on their way to Bethlehem they would have died Christians. Already in their hearts they were worshipping the Jesus they had not met.

Finally, every authentic act of faith is a *free choice* that involves the *risk* of personal decision.

In an act of faith the external evidence is never absolutely compelling. It may be logical — so logical, in fact, that to deny it is to deny the power of one's own intellect (as in the case of the arguments for the existence of God, for example). But in an act of faith there is always something more than the external evidence. There is the voice of God speaking in the heart. And no one can ever "prove," in any concrete, individual instance, that this voice really does or does not come from God. It simply has to be recognized (see *John* 10:3-5; 20:15-16; 21:4-7). That is why faith is never a conclusion, but always a free decision.

We can imagine how the magi must have argued among themselves — and each one within himself — when this new star appeared on their horizon. Was it a sign from God? Or was it just a comet, or some new, undiscovered planet?

Interiorly each one knew — because it was whispered to them by the Spirit speaking in their hearts — that this was an invitation from God. They knew it was a message, a sign. But they hesitated to believe what their hearts were telling them. How could they be sure? With their intellects they argued both sides of the question, and neither side was totally convincing. The evidence from the star alone was inconclusive. They had to decide whether or not to accept the evidence that was coming to them from within. The decision was up to them.

And this decision involved a lot of risk. Not to follow the star, if it was a sign from God, was to miss out on God's invitation. But to follow a star out into the desert, just on the possibility that it *might* be a sign from God, seemed a lack of common sense. How far would it lead them? How long would they be gone? When could they tell their wives they would return? And if it wasn't a sign from God, would they ever return at all? They wouldn't even know how much water to pack on their camels!

Like Abraham when he set out into the desert, and like Peter when he asked to walk on the water (Matthew 14:28), the astrologers had only one way of finding out for certain whether they were or were not being called by God: they just had to answer and see.

Not answer and see what happened. Just answer and see. It was in the act of answering that they knew. Peter knew in the instant of jumping out of the boat that the one calling him was Jesus. And the astrologers knew just as soon as they made their decision that the star they were following was from God. But they had to make that decision. And this is characteristic of every true act of faith: it is a free and personal act of choice.

This is the act of choice that every human being on earth was born to make. And God summons each one to it in different ways. This is what the story of the magi tells us: that the revelation of Jesus Christ comes to different people in different ways. God speaks to each individual in the language he or she is best prepared to understand, but always with an invitation to respond to the person of Jesus Christ.

And each one's response must be different. This is not to say that there is no such thing as a common response, or that those who believe in Jesus cannot be united in one community of faith: "one Lord, one faith, one baptism" (see *Ephesians* 4:5). But it means that even within the one community of faith each individual is called to respond to God in a manner appropriate to his or her own reality. Each one of us must answer with what we are.

We see this in the Gospels. The announcement of Christ's birth, for example, is made in the Gospels to some quite different categories of people. To each group it is made differently, and the response of each group is different.

The *astrologers* were educated men, but ignorant of God's revelation to the Jews. They were, however, devout. *Herod* was also educated, but unlike the astrologers, he was not ignorant of God's revelation; nor was he devout like they were. He knew the Scriptures but he did not live by them.

The *shepherds* (see *Luke* 2:8-20) were unlike both Herod and the astrologers through the fact that they were uneducated. But like the astrologers (and unlike Herod) they were devout. And like Herod (but unlike the astrologers) they knew the revelation made to Israel; they were believing Jews.

Finally, Jesus was also revealed to *Simeon and
Anna* in the Temple (see *Luke* 2:22-38). They too were
educated (in the ways of God, at least). They were
devout. And they were believers, familiar with God's
revelation. They belonged to the Chosen People.

To the astrologers, as we have seen, God sent His
message through a star. It was a sign they would
recognize. He spoke to them in the language of their
own religion. To the shepherds, however, He sent a
vision of angels. They were simple people, not used to
the subtleties of intellect or of discernment, and God
spoke to them simply and directly.

Herod was another case. Although he was a Jew,
acquainted with God's revelation to Israel and quite
possibly in his own mind a believer, he was not a man
whose faith could be appealed to. He was not really
centered on the things of God, or on the values of the
spirit, but on this world with its grosser pleasures and
its sophisticated illusions of power, importance and
prestige. So to him God sent the magi.

They were important people — tradition sometimes calls them "kings" — and they left royal gifts
with Jesus: gold, frankincense, and myrrh (*Matthew*
2:11). They were rich, they were sophisticated, and
they were learned. Herod was impressed.

The real message to Herod, though, was their
faith. They came to Herod's court in their wrappings
of sophistication and importance, which made them
acceptable, and laid the jewel of their faith before
him. They announced with the simplicity of children:
"Where is the newborn king of the Jews? We have
come to worship him."

The astrologers didn't hide behind a cynical
reserve, saying, "We've heard something about a possible king of the Jews who has been born, and we've

just come to check him out." That would have been
the sophisticated thing to do. But they came right out
with their profession of personal faith: "We have
come to worship him." And it sent Herod into a
frenzy. The fact that these men believed, and pro-
fessed their faith so openly, disturbed him. The
message had struck home (see *Matthew* 2:3).

Of all those who received the message of Christ's
birth, Simeon and Anna were the only ones who were
both instructed in the truth of God's revelation and
also given to a life of serious reflection and prayer. To
them God's messenger was the Holy Spirit Himself.
They were familiar with Him; they were accustomed
to listening for his voice in discernment and prayer.
And so when Jesus was brought into the Temple the
Spirit was able to enlighten them that they might
recognize the presence of God, not in angels or in a
star, but in the incarnate reality of Jesus Himself.

And each group of those who encountered Jesus
*responded* according to their own reality and condition. They all gave gifts appropriate to what they
were; gifts that expressed their own selves.

The shepherds simply gave praise. They returned
to their fields "glorifying and praising God for all they
had heard and seen, in accord with what had been
told them" (*Luke* 2:20). They were poor people,
simple people. They received God's gift and praised
Him for it. It was all they were asked to do.

What the astrologers gave was not more (see
*Luke* 21:3), but it was different. They were expected
to respond with what they had, and so they gave gifts
proportionate to their wealth: gold, frankincense and
myrrh. But more than this, they gave themselves: they
were converted. They were not asked to embrace the
Jewish religion, and Christianity had not yet taken

form. But having responded to the voice of God calling them to His Son, they could never walk again in
the way they used to follow. They returned to their
own country, but "by another route" (*Matthew* 2:12).

Herod's gift was murder. And it was according to
the reality that he was. The magi received the message
of Jesus' birth with discerning seriousness, struggling
between sceptical common sense and a faith that
opened into hope. The shepherds received the message with simple wonderment, fear and joy. But
when Herod heard the news he was "greatly disturbed." And "all Jerusalem" — all of Herod's own
circle, that is — was thrown into panic with him (see
*Matthew* 2:3). Jesus is "good news" in Himself; but
for many people the good news is bad news, and light
itself is darkness to them (see *John* 3:19-21).

And so Herod responded with the gift most
characteristic of himself, of the person he chose to be.
He sent his soldiers to massacre all the infants in
Bethlehem in the hope of destroying Jesus (*Matthew*
2:16).

The gift of Anna and Simeon was prophecy
(*Luke* 2:25-38). The lifestyle of both was characterized by familiarity with God in prayer and discernment. Luke says of Simeon, "the Holy Spirit was
upon him"; and of Anna that she was a "prophetess...
constantly in the temple, worshiping day and night in
fasting and prayer." Because of what they were, they
were able to bear witness to Christ as only the
prayerful can bear it, a witness "inspired by the
Spirit." And this was their gift to Him.

The Gospels show us, then, four different types
of people, including both believing Jews and pagans,
and ranging from the most devout to the most
corrupt. But the event of Jesus enters the life of them

all. The message comes to each in a different way, and each responds in a different way, according to each one's own reality and choice. But each is encountered by Jesus, and each one is summoned to respond.

The meaning of this is that Jesus — His Incarnation, His message, and the destiny He offers — is not a reality anyone can ignore. Everyone, sooner or later, is confronted by the fact of Jesus Christ. This is because Jesus is universal Lord. He is not just this or that culture's concept of divinity. He is not even God's particular way of revealing Himself to the people of one civilization. He is not a cultural or racial god, an ethnic expression of truth. He is not just the God of the Jews, the inspiration of western civilization, or that concept of the deity which most appeals to the Graeco-Roman mind. He is the light of God Himself come to earth in concrete form to be the light of the world: "the real light which gives light to every man" (*John* 1:9). He comes to all, and all who receive Him are "empowered to become children of God" (*John* 1:12). He is the Lord and the destiny of all.

"Why Jesus? Why take a stance toward Him?"
"Because it is impossible not to."

CHAPTER SIX: JESUS IS AN INESCAPABLE
QUESTION — *Matthew* 2:1-12

Summary:

1. Jesus was born to be Lord and shepherd of the whole human race. God calls all men to His Son, speaking to them in whatever language each can understand. Those who respond unconditionally in faith, "following their star," have "baptism of desire" and are responding in fact to Jesus Christ, whether they recognize Him or not.

2. Every authentic act of Faith must be like the astrologers' response to the star; i.e., it must be:

    a) an initiative from God, a movement of grace
    b) unconditional and open-ended
    c) a true, concrete human decision, responding to something definite (which in fact is Jesus Christ)
    d) an act of free choice, involving the risk of personal decision

3. In the stories of the astrologers, the shepherds, Herod, and Simeon and Anna we see four different types of people, each receiving the message of Christ's birth in a different way, each responding differently with a "gift" that expresses the reality of each. This tells us that every person, sooner or later, encounters Jesus Christ in some form or another. Every man and woman on earth must sooner or later make a decision in response to Jesus Christ. It is impossible not to.

*Questions for prayer and discussion:*

1. In what ways have I experienced God speaking within my heart? How has God led me to Jesus? To His Church? What "stars" has God sent to me?

2. Have I ever experienced making an act of faith that involved the risk of personal, free decision and choice? When I chose to act in faith, was my decision confirmed in any way?

3. What is my "gift" to Christ? What response do I make to Him that is the unique expression of what *I* am? What is *my* way of answering the Gospel?

4. This chapter invites me to reflect on my response of faith to Jesus Christ. What makes my own act of faith unconditional and open-ended? Am I committed to following any concrete "star" wherever it leads? Should I be?

## CHAPTER SEVEN

## JESUS IS A WAY OF GROWTH

*A transitional chapter: review and preview*

We have just studied the passages of Matthew that reveal to us one side of the saving mission of Jesus: who He is and what He came to do for us. Matthew has explained to us that Jesus is the promised "Son of David," the culmination of Jewish history and the goal and meaning of all human history. The ultimate meaning and value of every human life is measured by relationship with Christ. Our own reason for being on earth is to enter into relationship with Him and to contribute to "reestablishing all things in Christ." This is the enduring significance our "names" will have for all eternity.

Jesus is also the saving presence of God on earth. His name — "Jesus" — means "God saves." And He is called "Emmanuel," which means "God is with us." Jesus came to "save" human life, to bring it to authenticity and to fullness, by making available to men in a human way the perfect truth, values, attitudes and power of God. He not only saves us by making our lives authentically human; He also offers us the grace (favor) of sharing in the life of God: of living and functioning on the transcendent, supernatural level of God's own act of knowing, choosing and loving.

Because in Jesus God has become a man, it is possible for us now to base our whole lives on a human relationship with Jesus Christ. We can interact with Him in a human way. We can form our own personalities in response to His attitudes, values and initiatives in our lives. We can talk to Him, hear His words and reflect on their meaning. We can work for Him, serve Him and be served by Him as His disciples did and were when He was living among them. Everything Jesus did on earth for those who dealt with Him He still does today for those who continue to deal with Him in faith as with one who is risen and alive. The choice to base our whole lives on such interaction and relationship with Jesus is the basic content of the decision to be a Christian.

Jesus is the Lord and destiny of all men. In ways too many, too personal and too mysterious for us to know or categorize, God calls to relationship with His Son every man, woman and child who is born into this world. To respond to His voice is to follow the "star" He has sent us, determined in advance to accept and to surrender to all that God reveals. In our own case as Christians, Jesus Himself — living and teaching in His Church — has become our star.

This, then, is the mission of Jesus. What is my response to it? Is my life directed to reestablishing all things according to the pattern and ideals taught by Jesus? Am I shaping my personality — making the choices, forming the attitudes and values which will characterize me as a person — through conscious interaction with His mind and will? Am I basing my life on His teaching and example? Have I embraced Him as my destiny, the hope and fulfillment of my life? And have I accepted the guidance God has provided for me to lead me to deeper knowledge and love of Him?

If I were asked "Why Jesus?" what would my answer be now?

But there is another side to Jesus' saving mission on earth; a side that brings us into conflict and crisis. This also is redemptive, because it forces us to grow.

After the story of the astrologers, Matthew's Gospel takes a noticeable turn. Matthew begins to present Jesus as the "Suffering Servant" (see *Isaiah*, ch. 53) — a Savior who is paradoxically subject to weakness, persecution and apparent defeat. And not only that, but those whom He is saving suffer with Him.

How is this an incentive to seek relationship with Christ? What positive answer can we draw from this to our question, "Why Jesus?"

The answer is that because He is a suffering Savior, and because He allows us to suffer with Him, Jesus is a way of *growth*. He leads us to the fullness of life.

All who follow Jesus must advance or fall away (see *John* 15:2). And to advance means to rise to the level of God's own life and love. We must be made perfect as our heavenly Father is perfect (see *Matthew* 5:48), and the way to do this is to grow in likeness to Christ (*Colossians* 1:15 ff; 1 *Corinthians* 15:49). We must "put on" Christ (*Romans* 13:14) and adopt His attitude as our own (see *Philippians* 2:5-11).

To be conformed to Christ, however, is to be "formed into the pattern of his death" (*Philippians* 3:10). This is not as negative as it sounds. What "death" means for Christians is simply the passing to a higher level of existence. It can take place without physical death, and does take place everytime there is a "dying to self" on any level of our activity.

Every surrender of our intellects to God in faith, for example, is a dying to self. To "surrender our intellects" means, not that we stop using them (that would be to become less human), but just that we decide to accept as true whatever God tells us, regardless of how intelligible it may or may not appear to our own minds. When we accept God's word, and the example of Jesus Christ, and the voice of His Spirit within us as the light we choose to live by, we have in a sense "died" to the light of our human intellects as the final criterion of what we will and will not affirm. But by the same act we "live" to the light of God's own presence illuminating us from within.

Every time a pilot decides to trust his instruments instead of flying "by the seat of his pants," he "dies" in this same meaning of the word to his own natural sense of balance, distance, speed, etc.

Since God's light is brighter and clearer than our own, it is no diminishment to "die" to the light of our human intellects in order to walk by the light of faith. To do this is to see the truth more clearly, not less clearly — even though on the level of our minds and thoughts we may experience it as if we were not seeing at all.

To "walk by the light of faith" does not mean that we guide ourselves by something completely external to us, like a blind man following voice commands. It is true that we determine to live by God's written word in Scripture. But the "word" of God that we follow is not only written in the Bible; it is also being spoken in our hearts by the Holy Spirit. To surrender to God in faith does not mean we affirm as true something we do not know. It means we affirm as true something we know by a light other than that of our own human minds. But this light, the light of faith, is a light shining within us. It is God's light shared with us, God's vision shared with us, God's own act of knowing that we participate in.

When we follow God "blindly" in the "dark light of faith," we have the *effect* of vision without the sensation of seeing. In reality we know the truth we are walking by, and we know it with a certitude greater than any other. But since with our thoughts we cannot get a clear grasp on what we know, we sometimes experience this knowledge as if it were something completely exterior — even foreign — to us, something God sees and tells us about, but that we don't see at all.

This is why walking by faith can feel to us like dying. We experience it as "dying" to our natural way of knowing things in order to know by a way that is not natural to us — namely, by sharing in God's own act of knowing. And that is what faith is: a sharing in God's own divine act of knowing. It is the acceptance of a higher level of existence through "grace"; that is, through the "favor" of union with God. It is this union, this being joined with God through the gift of His indwelling presence, (see *John* 14:12-23), which allows us to participate, to actively share, in His own life and activity.

Our natures resist this. We are like people wading out into the ocean: when our weight begins to be taken by the water instead of resting on our own two feet, we experience that we are losing control. Then we want to go back to the shallows, where we can control our movements through feet that have a grip on the earth. It takes courage, and trust, to let oneself be lifted by the waves. It takes something like heroism, or trust that is absolute, to surrender oneself unconditionally to the ocean.

Yes this is what we are called to. God doesn't ask us to stop using our natures or our natural equipment. He just calls us out into the depths of His own life and activity where our natural equipment doesn't help us very much; and where it certainly doesn't give us control.

When He does this He is calling us into the mystery of death and resurrection in Christ: of "losing" life on one level to find it again on a higher level in God. Our physical deaths — our passage from earth to heaven, from this life to the "next" life — are just a visible manifestation of what already happened to us in baptism when we "died" to our isolated, human lives in order to live in Christ, as members of His Body (see *John* 12:24-25; 1 *Corinthians* 15:35-38; *Romans* 6:3-23). And every time we surrender more of ourselves, or surrender more deeply, to Christ and to His Spirit within us, we "die" more completely to ourselves to *live* more completely in Him. Our physical deaths are not a passage to "another" life — neither to the "next" life nor to the "life to come." They are simply total entrance into the life that is already ours.

Our sharing in God's life is experienced most basically on earth as a living by faith, hope and love. None of these is natural to us, because we are talking precisely about that faith, hope and love which are supernatural; i.e., which are a graced sharing in God's own life and activity. The more we are called to live purely by the light of God within us, which is faith; to trust purely in the power of God within us, which is hope; and to act purely by the love that is "poured out in our hearts through the Holy Spirit who has been given to us," the more resistance we feel in our natures. We fear to "let go" and be carried out into the deep.

It is to help us overcome this resistance that Christ comes to us as the "Suffering Servant." In the chapters that follow we will see how the saving mission of Jesus is not completely revealed to us until we recognize Him as the Savior who joins us to Himself in His human weakness in order to lead us to life-transcending death. This "death" is the total abandonment of ourselves to Him and to the Father in faith, in hope and in love.

As we continue to inquire "Why Jesus?" we will take up again the story of the astrologers, then the stories of the flight into Egypt and the massacre of the innocents of Bethlehem. Our focus will be on Jesus as the "Suffering Servant" who calls us through our experience of weakness to the acceptance of life in its fullness.

CHAPTER SEVEN: JESUS IS A WAY OF GROWTH —
A preview of *Matthew* 2:1-18

*Summary:*

1. To see Jesus as "Son of David," the fulfillment of God's promises and the meaning of human history: as "Jesus-Emmanuel," the "saving presence of God on earth"; as universal Lord and destiny of all mankind — this is only to see one half of His mission. To understand the fullness of His saving action in our lives, we must recognize Jesus as the "Suffering Servant."
2. By leading us into conflict — conflict with others, conflict with our own natural resistance to "letting go" and living fully by faith, hope and love, Jesus forces us to grow. He makes us confront dying to self as a passage to the fullness of life.
3. Divine life is not a diminishment of our natural lives. But because it is more than what is natural to us, and because it involves giving up control, we are afraid of it and we resist it.

Jesus helps us to overcome this resistance by associating us with Himself in the weakness of His humanity.

*Questions for prayer and discussion:*

1. When have I experienced the grace of faith, hope and love most purely as *gift*? Was it when I was strong, confident and in control of the situation? Or when I was weak, frightened and conscious of my helplessness?

2. What do I find most painful, or most difficult, in acting by pure faith? Have I ever had to do this? When? Have I ever had to trust in God alone, with nothing else to trust in? Was it painful? Did it lead me to a deeper, more absolute sense of security?

3. Have I ever done anything for God purely and simply out of love? That is, without any motivation from fear or from hope of reward? What could I do that would be such an act?

4. This chapter raises the question of going beyond our natural level of life — our natural way of knowing, our natural sources of confidence, our natural incentives to love — in order to let God raise us to the level of His own divine life and activity. Am I willing at this point to look positively on this? Can I desire it? Can I ask Him for it?

## CHAPTER EIGHT

## JESUS IS THE "CRISIS" OF HUMAN LIFE

In the story of the astrologers (*Matthew* 2:1-12) Jesus already begins to appear as the "Suffering Servant" — at least in the sense that He is a source of conflict and division. His coming calls people into crisis. Everyone to whom the news of His birth is announced must respond either with joy and faith like the astrologers (*Matthew* 2:10) or with disturbance and rejection like Herod (*Matthew* 2:3). This story, then, invites us to see Jesus as the one who requires us to grow to the maturity of graced life through decisions increasingly based on faith. By calling us into "crisis" — and specifically into progressively deeper crises of faith — Jesus leads us to the fullness of graced, supernatural life.

The story of the astrologers presents Jesus as universal Lord and destiny of all mankind. But this does not mean that everyone will find Him acceptable. The story of the magi shows us that the coming of Jesus into the world causes conflict and division (see also *Luke* 2:34; 12:49-53; *John* 1:10-12; *Matthew* 10:34-36). Not all men want what Jesus came to offer. For some He is good news; for others He is bad news.

When the astrologers arrived in Jerusalem with the news of Christ's birth, Matthew tells us that "King Herod became greatly disturbed, and with him all Jerusalem." The astrologers, on the other hand, when they saw the star reappear after having lost it, were "overjoyed" (*Matthew* 2:3, 10; see also *Luke* 2:34; *John* 1:10-12; *Matthew* 10:34-36).

Not all men want what Jesus came to offer. For some He is good news; for others He is bad news. For all, however, He is a "crisis," a dividing point. His entry into our lives faces us with a decision from which and through which we either go up or go down.

We have already seen that sooner or later every human person encounters Jesus or is called to Him by some "star." Once God takes the initiative in calling, we must answer with a yes or a no. There is no middle ground: not to say yes to God is to say no. We might delay and put off our answer, even for years; and God is a patient God. But sooner or later all of us must accept Christ or reject Him, embrace Him as our destiny or seek our fulfillment elsewhere.

We see already in this the pressure that is on us to grow. Our first reaction to this fact about Jesus may be that we do not want to encounter Him, because we do not want to come into crisis. We do not want to be faced with any fundamental decision about ourselves, our lives, or God. Above all, we do not want to be faced with a decision in faith. And therefore we avoid encounter with Christ.

To refuse the crisis of choice, however, is to refuse the level of authentic human existence. Our free response to life — to ourselves, to other people and to God — is what creates us as unique, individual persons. Our choices determine who we are; they carve out the shape of our souls. And the choice that determines most decisively who we are is the response we make to the person of Jesus Christ.[1]

Salvation, although it is a free gift from God, is not accomplished without deep, all-embracing, radical choices on our part. God requires us to choose, and He makes the achievement of our destiny depend on the exercise of our free choice. By this He summons us to the fullness of human as well as divine life (see chapter 4 above). For us to refuse freedom and the responsibility of making choices is to refuse both God and the dignity of being human. They go together. We must accept our humanity in its authentic fullness if we are to respond to God. We can only be surrendered to God and to His saving grace in an act of taking responsibility for ourselves. We can only be united to Him or "put on Christ" in an act of becoming ourselves.

The astrologers had to decide whether or not to believe that the star they saw was a sign from God. God didn't come in power and majesty to convince them. He didn't overwhelm their minds with the clarity of His light. He came in the weakness and the littleness of a messenger they were able to refuse. He left them free to choose whether or not they would believe.

This is usually the case when God sends us a sign. He leaves us a way to deny that the message comes from Him. He wants us to believe in Him because we choose to, not because our intellects can find no escape. Faith is a free choice; it is offered as a gift but never forced upon us.

At the same time, our response to God's invitation is our "judgment." We are free to accept or to refuse His gift, but we are not free to deny what our acceptance or refusal says about us, or what it causes

us to become. If the entrance of Jesus into our lives
disturbs us, and if we respond with an effort to get rid
of Him, like Herod did, then this tells us something
about ourselves. If, on the other hand, we respond to
Him (after a struggle, perhaps) with joy, this also is a
"judgment" on our lives — one we can be glad of.

In Greek the word for "judgment" is *krisis* —
from which our English word "crisis" comes. By being
the "crisis" point in our lives Jesus is also our judgment. Our encounter with Him forces us to choose.
The response we make to Jesus when we finally
encounter Him (which may be, not once, but several
times: see *John* 1:29, 35), is the turning-point and the
revelation of our existence: through it we both discover and determine who we are (see *John* 3:17-21;
9:39; 12:31, 44-48). It is by choosing or not choosing
Christ as our destiny that we create ourselves ultimately as the persons we will be for all eternity.

When we ask, "Why Jesus?" then; and more particularly, why a Jesus who brings us into crisis, the
answer is, "Because that is the only way we can grow."
Jesus forces us to face the deep questions of life (see
*John* 1:38). By confronting us with His own reality,
with our power and our need to make a choice, and
with the consequences of whatever choice we make,
He obliges us to face the question both of our
humanity and of our call to be divine.

Specifically, by putting us in a position where we
must freely choose whether to believe or not to believe
in Him, He summons us to accept the light of faith,
which is a sharing in God's own knowledge and life.

Why Jesus? In a word, because He *calls us to life*.
And to *live* is to live by faith.

> Eternal life is this:
> to *know you*, the only true God,
> and him whom you have sent, Jesus Christ.
> (*John* 17:3)

*FOOTNOTE*

¹For more development of the ideas in this paragraph, see my books: *The Good News About Sex*, chapter 5: "A Person Is A Chosen Stance" (St. Anthony Messenger Press, 1979); and *His Way*, chapter 2: "The Person of Christ In Your Life" (St. Anthony Messenger Press, 1977).

## CHAPTER EIGHT: JESUS IS THE "CRISIS" OF HUMAN LIFE — *Matthew* 2:1-12

*Summary:*

1. Sooner or later, every one of us encounters Jesus or is called to Him by some "star." Everyone answers with a "Yes" or a "No." There is no middle ground with Christ. Not to say "Yes" is to say "No." We are often afraid to take the responsibility of life-determining choices, but there is no other way to respond to the grace of Jesus Christ. Encounter with Christ forces us to accept or refuse both our human level of life (with the dignity of freedom that goes with it) and the offer of sharing in the life of God.

2. Our immediate *reaction* to encounter with Jesus (His word, His ideals, His action in our lives) manifests itself as either disturbance (*Matthew* 2:3) or joy (*Matthew* 2:10). This reaction tells us whether we perceive Christ (or His invitation to us) as fulfillment or as threat. And this tells us something about ourselves. (There are, however, different kinds of disturbance: see *Luke* 1:29).

3. The *response* we make to Christ (not reaction, but free choice) both *reveals* and *determines* who we are and whom we choose to be. All our choices create us as persons. We create our ultimate, individual reality by the choice we make (or refuse to make) of Jesus as our destiny.

4. Our response to Jesus is always a free act of faith. We must *choose* to believe that it is really He whom we have met or that it is God who is calling us through our "star." It will always be possible for us to deny it. Faith is a free choice. It is offered as a gift but never forced upon us.

5. This is why Jesus is called the "judgment" (in Greek *krisis*, from which our English word "crisis" comes). He is the crisis point in our lives. Our response to Him is our judgment, and a judgment pronounced on the real orientation of our lives up to that point (see *John* 3:19; 9:39). Some people in the midst of sin are longing for deliverance. Others in the midst of apparently religious lives are indifferent or opposed to the

ideals of Christ. When we respond to the reality of His intervention in our lives the truth of our hearts is revealed (see *Luke* 2:35).

*Questions for prayer and discussion:*

1. What choices have I had to make in my life which were in reality a choice to believe or not to believe that Jesus was speaking to me?
2. What have I learned about myself from the times I have been "turned off" or angered when confronted with a higher ideal? Have I ever refused to follow when my heart was moving and inspiring me to something higher, just because I didn't have the courage to believe this was from God?
3. Have I experienced Jesus as a "crisis" in my life? — i.e., as an encounter with God or God's truth from which I had to either go up or go down? Which way did I go? How have I felt about it since?
4. This chapter invites me to take responsibility for creating my own being through choices. Have I done that? And in particular, have I done that with regard to the choice to put my faith in Jesus Christ?

## CHAPER NINE

## JESUS IS SECURITY IN GOD ALONE

In the story of the flight into Egypt (*Matthew* 2:13-15) Matthew presents Jesus to us as one who leads us to an ever-deepening reliance on God alone in hope. Our association with Him in His weakness forces us to ask what strength we really trust in, and where our true security, our absolute good, is found.

After the astrologers had left, Matthew tells us that "an angel of the Lord suddenly appeared in a dream to Joseph with the command: 'Get up, take the child and his mother, and flee to Egypt. Stay there until I tell you otherwise. Herod is searching for the child to destroy him'" (*Matthew* 2:13).

To us this warning might seem to be a marvellous proof of God's protection. But to Mary and Joseph, who found themselves after it fleeing into exile in the middle of the night, political exiles, poor and without friends in a foreign land, it must have seemed quite otherwise. If Jesus was the Messiah, and the Son of the Most High God (see *Luke* 1:32-35), why is it that Jesus and His parents were doing the running? Why didn't God send His angel to Herod instead and strike him dead? In the time of King Hezekiah, when the Assyrian army was threatening Jerusalem, one angel working alone struck down five thousand men in the Assyrian camp in a single night (see 2 *Kings* 19:35). That's protection! Why, then, did Mary and Joseph have to flee?

If to be a follower of Jesus means to be on the losing end all of one's life — to be with the weak and the poor and the persecuted, and apparently without the favor and protection of God — then again we are tempted to ask, "Why Jesus? Who needs a Savior who has to run away to be saved?"

The answer lies again in the mystery of the "Suffering Servant": the Savior who saves by joining us to Himself in what appears to be nothing but poverty, weakness and defeat. And He does this to make us grow.

We are very shortsighted about God's help to us. Or else we are exclusively farsighted. We take being "saved" to mean either deliverance from all the immediate things that threaten us here on earth (sickness, poverty, persecution, etc.) — and this is the shortsighted view — or else we take it to mean nothing at all short of getting to heaven when we die — and this is the exclusively farsighted view. In either case we miss the meaning of salvation and the role of Jesus as Savior.

Salvation is in the now. It goes on forever, of course, but it begins right here on earth. Jesus saves our lives and our existence here on earth — and what He gives to save us on earth is the very same thing that constitutes our ecstatic fulfillment in heaven. He doesn't give us one thing on earth and another in heaven. It is one and the same thing. And this is what we have to set our hopes on — not only hereafter but *here*. We have to make our happiness here and now consist in what will be our perfect joy forever. We have to re-focus our hopes, centering all our desire both in this life and in the next on one reality: *grace*, or the "favor of sharing life with God."

It is our *lives*, our existence, that Jesus saves. And the life we live on earth by grace, the life we *experience* here and now through the favor of union with God, this same life is our treasure, our beatitude, the perfect joy we experience in heaven. On earth our lives are not pure and perfect happines because we are not able to live or to experience purely and perfectly the life of God which has been given to us. But what we experience of the life of God right now (our sharing in which we call "grace") is a foretaste of heaven itself.[1]

All of this seems very unreal to us, however. What we know we want is *happiness*. And we all tend to identify happiness with various concrete things, such as prosperity, friendships, good health, success and the like. Anything that threatens to take these things away from us frightens us and makes us insecure. Anything that gives us these things — with some assurance we can hold on to them — makes us complacent.

And that's the problem.

The more our physical and psychological needs are satisfied, the more we tend to think we "have it made." We see ourselves as satisfied, our lives as enjoyable, our existence as fulfilled. We have heard that heaven will be even better, of course, and that pleases us, like the prospect of an exquisite dessert after a delightful meal. But heaven is for later. Everything we are really interested in is before us here and now. We want "all this" that we are naturally attracted to on earth "and heaven too." In other words, we want two salvations; we define happiness on earth in one way, and happiness in heaven in another.

It's all illusion, of course. The fact is, nothing on earth can really make us happy, and anything that does we can't hold onto. There is no real security — not from health, not from wealth, not from the friends we have. Jesus taught this when He said, "Do not lay up for yourselves an earthly treasure. Moths and rust corrode; thieves break in and steal. Make it your practice instead to store up heavenly treasure..." (*Matthew* 6:19-20).

Our only true security is in God — not in the fact that God provides health and prosperity and success for us, but *just in God*. God is our true happiness; not the things God supplies us with, but God Himself. Our true and perfect joy, both on earth and in heaven, is in the possession of God. This is the core of Jesus' preaching.

Jesus lost no time in teaching us this. Before He was two years old His parents were learning that the coming of the promised Messiah did not mean for them either comfort or wealth or immunity from oppression. Jesus was not that kind of Savior. God showed them early — and showed us through them — that not only will Jesus and His followers be persecuted, but God will not use His power to defend them. He will leave them frightened, weak, and apparently abandoned to their enemies, with no other recourse than to run away. God sends an angel to warn Joseph and Mary it is time to flee, but nothing more.

Jesus doesn't want us to set our hopes on a salvation He doesn't promise — not because He will not at times procure for us prosperity or friends or escape from our enemies, but because He wants us to focus both our minds and our hearts on the salvation He really *does* promise. He doesn't want us settling for less.

This is why He frequently leaves us weak and subject to oppression. It is the only way to make us face the fact — and it is a glorious fact — that He offers us a happiness and a salvation that are not dependent on what we have or do not have in this world, or on what any human being may be for us, do to us or do against us. He offers us Himself to be our joy now and forever.

Before we can re-focus our desires on Jesus alone, however, and seek our happiness in Him in any way that is real, we have to "die" to all we identify as happiness here on earth. This doesn't mean we have to give it up, it just means we have to stop depending on it. Jesus never taught, for example, that people are *better* if they are poor; just that they are better off. This is because sometimes the only way we can learn to stop depending on something is just to be without it for awhile.

When Jesus came in poverty and weakness He set us the example of a life lived in total dependence on God. His purpose in doing this was not to deprive us of anything; it was to open our hearts to the "more" He came to give.

That "more" is the all-fulfilling happiness of grace.

And when He was left without the apparent favor and protection of the Father, this was to teach us not to base our trust in God on what He does for us, but simply on who He is. The flight into Egypt was just a beginning; the most absolute experience Jesus had of abandonment by His Father came on the cross when He cried out, "My God, my God, why have you forsaken me?" (*Matthew* 27:46). But it was through these experiences that Jesus Himself learned what it means to trust absolutely in the Father (see also *Hebrews* 5:8). And when we also are left without any sign or proof whatsoever of God's favor and protection, then we are challenged to grow. It is in our moments of abandonment that we learn who God really is for us and that nothing He does or fails to do can be a denial of His love. No matter how forsaken we may feel, we know He is our Father and our God.

Why Jesus? Why a Savior who has to flee in poverty and weakness before His enemies?

Because this Jesus is the one who teaches us absolute hope in God.

### FOOTNOTE

[1]Grace, or the favor of sharing God's life, is already essentially heaven. But the God we possess by grace is not perfectly experienced in this life. In the measure that He is we call this "union." St. John of the Cross compares the possession of God through grace to betrothal and His possession through union to marriage. The difference lies in the manner and degree of *communication*. (See *Living Flame Of Love*, Stanza II, parag. 24)

CHAPTER NINE:  JESUS IS SECURITY IN GOD ALONE —
*Matthew* 2:13-15

*Summary:*

1. Mary and Joseph must flee into Egypt with the child. Anyone associated with Jesus must expect persecution. Prestige and power are not promised to Christ's followers; nor is success as the world judges success. But "in weakness power reaches perfection" (2 *Corinthians* 12:9).
2. The experience of persecution and weakness can nurture spiritual growth. It calls forth total faith and trust in God by stripping us of every other source of security. It confirms that trust when God protects us in spite of dangers, and does so without reliance on human power (e.g., the angel's warning to Joseph, the escape).

3. Insecurity and deprivation can help us to realize that true salvation — and true happiness — are not to be identified with the satisfaction of any or all of our earthly needs. We are not made ultimately happy, nor is our existence saved, by health, wealth, achievement, or even human relationships. This realization empowers us to set our hope on God alone as our true destiny and beatitude.

4. More deeply yet, when God leaves us without any experience of His favor, His protection or His gifts, this makes it possible for us to surrender in faith to God Himself as love. When there is no created expression of God's love to respond to, we can learn what it is to accept God as love absolute, uncreated and unconditional. This is pure, supernatural love.

*Questions for prayer and discussion:*

1. What is my hope, my trust in God, dependent on? Have I ever been tempted to think God was punishing me, or didn't care about me, because He allowed me to experience hardship, suffering or failure? What is it in Scripture that I can fall back on and believe in at such times?

2. What do I in fact aim at in order to be happy on earth? Do I think happiness (on earth) is dependent on health, possessions, success, certain human relationships? Are there two kinds of happiness to aim at: one that we can have during this life, and another that we can have after death? If happiness is the same here and hereafter, what does it consist in?

3. Have I ever had the experience of trusting in God just because He is God? Not because of *what* He is doing for me, but just because of *who* He is? If I have had this experience, what brought me to it?

4. This chapter invites me to decide that I will trust absolutely in God, just because of who He is, regardless of what signs He gives or does not give me of His favor. This is a radical decision. Am I ready to make it? If not, what decision can I make as an approach to it?

## CHAPTER TEN

## JESUS IS THE TOTAL GIFT OF SELF

In the story of the astrologers we see Jesus challenging us to rise above the natural light of reason to walk by that supernatural light which belongs to Him alone, but which He shares with us by grace. He calls us to this through the "crisis" of many free acts of decision in faith.

The flight into Egypt serves us notice that a life spent in association with Jesus the "Suffering Servant" will inevitably demand of us absolute trust in the person of God and a radical refocusing of all our desires on the blessing of His Kingdom alone (see *Matthew* 6:19-34; 8:19-22; 10:21-39; 16:24-28). This is the perfection of supernatural hope.

Now, in the story of the innocents of Bethlehem (*Matthew* 2:16-18), Matthew presents Jesus as one who calls us to the height of supernatural love.

St Paul wrote, "There are in the end three things that last: faith, hope, and love, and the greatest of these is love" (1 *Corinthians* 13:13). When Matthew reports the massacre of the innocents by Herod, he shows God calling us through Jesus to the peak of this graced love. The massacre of the innocents forces us to ask just how much Jesus is worth to us. Is the life

He offers worth the sacrifice of life itself? (see *Matthew* 13:44-46; 16:24-26).

When the astrologers did not report back to Herod where Jesus was to be found, Matthew tells us that Herod became furious. "He ordered the massacre of all the boys two years old and under in Bethlehem and its environs" (*Matthew* 2:16).

We think immediately of Jesus' words:

There is no greater love than this:
to lay down one's life for one's friends (*John* 15:13)

In the case of the innocents of Bethlehem, however, those who are "laying down their lives" are infants. How could God possibly ask them — and how could they understand that He was asking them — to accept being massacred in the place of His Son? And what does it say to us that little children died while the Savior escaped unharmed?

There is no explanation for all this unless dying for Jesus, even while still an infant, can be a greater blessing than continuing in life. And dying can only be such a blessing if it is, in fact, an entrance into a fullness of life and of being that is more desirable than life itself.

But this doesn't mean what it suggests to us.

There is something too easy — and still unsatisfying — about explaining away the death of the innocents by saying, "They got something better: they went to heaven." Something in us feels that these babies should have had a chance to *live*. To die as they did is like being transported from the start to the finish line without any experience of running the race. They seem to have missed out on the adventure of human life, even if they received the same reward. Is the reward worth the same if you haven't gone through the risk and the excitement of struggling for it?

It is unfortunate that we speak of "heaven" as the goal and reward of human life. "Heaven" sounds like a place. It suggests to us a happiness that comes from our environment rather than from something within us; from *where* we are rather than from *what* we are.

But the reward and goal of the human drama is not to be somewhere; it is to *be*. Jesus came that we might have *life*, and have it in its fullness (*John* 10:10). To reach the fullness of life we have to grow and mature, have experiences, make choices, form attitudes and values, create our own personalities through response to the world around us and to God. The fullness of human life is not something anyone can hand us; it is a fullness of having lived. It is not something separate from ourselves that we receive; it is what we *are*, and we have to grow into it.

There is a recognition of this — implicit, at least — in the Scriptural association of a *full* life with a *long* life (*Exodus* 20:12; *Deuteronomy* 20:18; *Proverbs* 3:16; *Psalms* 21:5 and 91:16). Life is something one lives. The only way to have it fully is to live it fully; and normally that takes time.

Already in the old Testament, however, there was a recognition that the essential element in growing to the fullness of life is not in how long you live, but in how fast you develop.

> But the just man, though he die
>     early, shall be at rest.
> For the age that is honorable
>     comes not with the passing of time,
> nor can it be measured in
>     terms of years.
> Rather, *understanding* is the
>     hoary crown for men,

and an *unsullied life* the
attainment of old age. (*Wisdom* 4:7-9)

And the passage goes on to say of the just man who
dies young: "Having *become perfect* in a short while,
he reached the *fullness* of a long career."

The question is, how can a person while still a
baby become anything at all in terms of interior
growth? Can an infant reach what the Scriptures
mean by "*understanding*"? And the "unsullied life"
which is called the "attainment of old age" must be an
innocence that is *attained*. It certainly can't mean just
that purity of heart which is nothing but the absence
of temptation, freedom, or desire, which is what we
find in little babies. An "unsullied life" is not an
attainment or a level of personal growth until it is the
fruit of free and deliberate choice. And how can an
infant have this?

Let us begin by affirming the fact. *How* it can be
is another question, which we will also try to answer.
But *that* an infant can receive grace, choose Christ,
merit heaven, and respond to God with supernatural
faith, hope and love is not even open to question. It is
the Church's belief. This belief is expressed both in
the practice, dating back to the earliest centuries, of
granting baptism to infants, and in the fact that the
Church celebrates the death of the "holy innocents"
massacred by Herod as a martyrdom and considers
the Innocents themselves to be saints.

Obviously there is more to the massacre of the
Innocents than meets the eye. The infants of Bethlehem were not just children of two years old and under
who happened to be murdered. We celebrate them as
martyrs and as saints. This means that they weren't
just killed; they *offered* themselves. They reached the
fullness of life on earth in the act of making a *total gift*

*of themselves in love* to Jesus Christ. "There is no greater love than this: to lay down one's life for one's friends" (*John* 15:13). If the Innocents are saints and martyrs, then they laid down their lives for Jesus; and they did so as a personal act of love. They didn't just lose their lives; they gave their lives. And they gave them for Jesus in supernatural faith, hope and love. Their death was a free act — an act of free acceptance in which their full potentiality for love and self-gift reached perfection. They lost nothing of the experience of life. In their short life-span God brought them to that fullness of life and love which is the goal of all human living. They reached the perfection of love.

The saints are held up as models. The difference between those people we call "saints" and the rest of Christ's followers who are, as a matter of fact, made holy by the favor of sharing in God's own life which we call "grace" (and whom St. Paul routinely refers to as the "saints" or the "holy ones" — see *Romans* 12:13; 15:31; 1 *Corinthians* 16:15; *Ephesians* 2:19; *Colossians* 1:4) is that the saints are presented to us as examples of heroic response to the Gospel. They are held up to us as striking examples of what Christianity is all about, and as models for us to imitate.

The "Holy Innocents," then, are not just victims but heroes. They *attained* that "unsullied life" and measure of "understanding" which the Book of Wisdom identifies with the "attainment of old age." And what they did, we are invited to imitate.

What did they do?

There is only one thing that the attainment of an "unsullied life" can mean. If we are talking about that purity of heart and life which is a personal, chosen stance (as opposed to just the absence of temptation, awareness or opportunity), then "innocence" is synonymous with love. An "unsullied life" is a life so totally centered on Jesus Christ in love that no other desire can compete with one's total dedication to Him.

To be "pure of heart" means to be *single-hearted*. The phrase in the Scriptures can be translated this way (see *Matthew* 5:8, for example: "Blest are the single-hearted for they shall see God" and *Philippians* 1:17) because "pure" means simply "unmixed." The pure of heart, then, are those whose motivation is unmixed; the "single-hearted"; those who have set their hearts on the "one thing" that is necessary (see *Luke* 10:42); who have withdrawn their desires from everything else to center them solely on Jesus and the "pearl of great price" He offers (see *Matthew* 13: 44-46); and who follow His exhortation to seek first the Kingdom of God and His way of holiness (see *Matthew* 6:33), trusting that everything else will be supplied.

This is what the Innocents did. This is why they are held up to us as examples.

To give up life itself for Jesus is the most total and final way to love Him with our whole hearts. And this is what every one of us is called to do. We are called to make our act of dying a "martyrdom," that is, a *witness* to the faith we have in Jesus Christ ("martyr" in Greek just means "witness"), by freely accepting our death, however it may come to us, and *embracing* it as the means to make a total offering of ourselves to God in love.

This is what Matthew calls us to through the story of the massacred Innocents. He lets us know at the very beginning of his Gospel that the goal Jesus holds out to us is the perfection of love. And this perfection of love is the fullness of life.

We still are bothered by the question, "How could little babies make a free offering of themselves to Christ in love?" The Innocents weren't old enough to know what they were doing. They didn't understand what was happening to them, so how could they accept it or embrace it?

I wouldn't attempt to explain how, or even whether, God raised these infants at the moment of their death to some *psychological* level of maturity equal to that of adults. An individual's psychological functioning depends on many things, beginning with his physical condition. But no *person* is simply identified with his or her psychological functioning. Our reality, our being, and the basic human powers that are ours as human beings are not simply and totally dependent on our physical and mental ability to function at any given moment of our lives. In heaven people are not classified as infantile, adult, or senile. Those who died, or whose lives were terminated for them, while they were still physically undeveloped are not "sub-human" in heaven. Those whose age and hardened arteries have deprived them of rationality on earth are not "incompetents" in heaven. In heaven people are people, and God who embraces the beginning and the end of our lives is able to deal with all of us, all of the time, as the basic human beings that we are. He is able to by-pass our equipment.

We saw in chapter four above that God does not normally act in us unless we in some way cooperate with Him by the use of our human powers. God respects our humanity. When he joins Himself to us by grace, it is not to sweep our human natures aside and "take over," but to bring our human activity itself up to the level of His divine activity. We have to act *with* Him, as free and responsible human beings, in order to act by grace.

God's respect for our humanity does not mean, however, that God's power to act in us is *limited* by the condition of our natural equipment. Whenever no violation of our freedom is involved, God can grant us knowledge and love beyond anything our natures are capable of. Paul bore witness to this when he wrote:

> I know a man in Christ who, fourteen years ago, whether he was in or outside of his body I cannot say, only God can say — a man who was snatched up to the third heaven. I know that this man — whether in or outside his body I do not know, God knows — was snatched up to Paradise to hear words which cannot be uttered, words which no man can speak. (2 *Corinthians* 12:2-4)

What Paul saw and heard in this mystical experience no human being could see or hear anyway, no matter how developed his intellect might be, so God did not ignore Paul's human nature by acting in him this way. When Paul says he was "snatched up to Paradise," what he means is that God let Paul *experience*, in a measure beyond all natural competence, something of that divine life which God was living in him, and which Paul was already participating in by grace. This experience was so far beyond our human way of knowing or loving that Paul was unable to say whether he was "in or outside his body."

But what is true of mystical experience is just as true of the smallest act we perform by grace. To know and love God by grace — "supernaturally" — means to know and love God in a way that is utterly beyond the power of any created thing; in a way that is proper to God alone. The point is, there is *no* graced act, whether we are aware of it or not, which does not take

us utterly beyond what human nature is capable of.
St. Paul reminds us that no one can ever say "Jesus is
Lord," and believe it, except by the power of the Holy
Spirit (see 1 *Corinthians* 12:3). It is even more
impossible that anyone should be able to say "Jesus is
Lord" by the witness of embracing death itself out of
love for Him unless this is by the power of God.

We are asking the wrong question. The real
question is not how little babies, still physically and
psychologically immature, could accept death for
Jesus in an act of supernatural faith and hope and
love. The real question is how anybody can.

We don't become better able to love God with
our whole hearts because our minds are developed!
Jesus made that quite clear when He said:

> Father, Lord of heaven and earth, to you I offer
> praise; for what you have hidden from the learned
> and the clever you have revealed to the merest
> children. (*Matthew* 11:25)

The simple truth is, "*no one* knows the Son but the
Father, and *no one* knows the Father but the Son —
and anyone to whom the Son wishes to reveal him"
(*Matthew* 11:27). And therefore, what the story of the
Innocents tells us is that nothing whatsoever can
prevent God from giving Himself in faith, in hope and
in love to any one of His human creatures, no matter
how tiny, undeveloped or retarded; how sick, psychologically conditioned or sinful, if only that person is
willing in the deepest core of His being to say "Yes" to
the invitation of grace.

The fact is that God granted these babies the
grace, the favor of that union with Himself which
made it possible for them to share in God's own life
and activity even while their human powers were undeveloped. And so the love by which they offered

themselves to God in death was a love "poured out in their hearts through the Holy Spirit" who was given to them. It was not limited by their own human ability to know and love, but was a sharing in the knowledge and the love of Christ Himself.

By their "baptism of blood" they became members of Christ: His Body. In this baptism they "offered their bodies as a living sacrifice, holy and acceptable to God" (see *Romans* 12:1) and their bodies became Christ's Body. And so when they died at the hands of their executioners they didn't die in the place of the Savior; they died together with Him and He died in them.

Through this story Matthew teaches us not to judge God, His love or His providence by human appearances. We cannot measure the activity of God by our human measures. The sacrifice of the Innocents teaches us that even the ultimate sacrifice, the sacrifice of life itself, is meaningful and a blessing in the service of Christ, because it is an act by which we attain the fullness of life and of love.

This is the core message of the Gospel: that life sacrificed for Christ is not lost but its meaning found, its value realized. This is the response of love that matches the reality of God, the response in which we know that we love Him for what He really is: our God and our All. God, and the possession of God by grace, is not a partial good for man, but our total fulfillment. Appropriate love for God, then, gives all for All.

Why Jesus? Because as the "Suffering Servant," He leads us to the perfection of supernatural life in love.

## CHAPTER TEN: JESUS IS THE TOTAL GIFT OF SELF —
*Matthew* 2:16-18

*Summary:*

1. The massacre of the innocents shows us at the very beginning of the Gospel that response to Christ involves the total gift of self in love — including the surrender of one's whole life. Persecution or martyrdom with Jesus the "Suffering Servant" helps make us aware of what the acceptance of grace (dying and rising in Christ through baptism) really implies.

2. When we see that we or others are asked to give "all for All" in response to Jesus Christ, it helps us realize how great are the blessings of the Kingdom. To know and possess God, and be united with Him through grace, is worth every sacrifice, even the loss of life itself. The price we find ourselves (or others) willing to pay reveals to us the worth of what we believe in.

3. The fact that those who lay down their lives for Christ in this story are infants brings home to us that the love by which we love Jesus is a free gift of grace. It is that supernatural love, that sharing in the love of God Himself, which is "poured out in our hearts through the Holy Spirit who has been given to us" (*Romans* 5:5). Thus it is not a love limited by our human maturity or powers. Even the infants who died unconsciously for Christ (on the visible, psychological level at least) are celebrated as saints and martyrs. These are examples of "baptism of blood."

4. This story also teaches us that the fullness of life is not just something given to us; it is a fullness of living, of personal experience and response. The happiness of heaven comes from what we *are* and have become (through sharing in God's life), not from *where* we are. Therefore this happiness is something we have to *grow into* through our acts of personal response. To enjoy perfectly God's life in heaven, which is love, we have to become perfectly loving. The fullness of divine life is a gift; but it is at the same time a fullness of personal growth.

*Questions for prayer and discussion:*

1. Do I really believe that the gift of grace (union with God by sharing in His life) is worth every sacrifice I can make for it? What proof of this belief can I find in my concrete choices? What losses am I risking right now by decisions I have made to follow Christ's ideals in my professional (or student) life? In my social life? In my family life? In my civic or political involvement?

2. What do I identify as the fullness of life on this earth? Do my choices reflect what I say or think I believe about this? What concrete choices do or do not reflect this?

3. What concrete experience do I have of loving God or other people in a way that is beyond my human capacity? Are there things I do or desire which I cannot explain except through the gift of the Holy Spirit loving and longing within me?

4. This chapter invites me to love Jesus with the love that "sells all" for the sake of the treasure hidden in the field, the pearl of great price (see *Matthew* 13:44-46). It invites me to believe that Jesus is All and worth the sacrifice of all. Am I able to choose Him now with this fullness of faith, hope and love? Do I desire to be able to do this? Why?

*CHAPTER ELEVEN*

*JESUS IS VICTORY*

In the stories of the astrologers, the flight into Egypt, and the massacre of the Innocents, Matthew shows us that Jesus does not "make things easy" for those who follow Him. On the contrary, He challenges us to face decisions and to be ourselves more deeply; to grow to the maturity of human and divine life; and to "be made perfect" in faith, hope and love until we reach the fullness of graced, supernatural life.

Jesus doesn't deal with us as if we were fundamentally helpless and hopeless, and just do everything for us like an over-indulgent parent who is convinced his children will never grow up. Jesus does save us with the power of God. But He saves us in such a way that we are required to rise to the level of God Himself in our own human acts of knowing, loving and choosing. We cannot respond to Christ or persevere in our following of Him without being summoned to higher and higher levels of faith, hope and love.

The fullness of life is love, and the fullness of love is self-gift. Jesus asks the total gift of ourselves. His love, His desire for us embraces everything we are. He desires and He asks that everything we are be given and dedicated to Him. He asks all. And He is able to ask for all because He gives all. He is All. In Him we find one who is worth — and who is able to call forth — the bestowal of everything we are. Given to Him, the precious trust of our existence is finally well-used.

Jesus is the answer to the cry Christopher Fry writes into his play *Sleep Of Prisoners*:

O God, the fabulous wings unused,
Folded in the heart. . . .

The human heart can go to the lengths of God.
Dark and cold we may be, but this
Is no winter now. The frozen misery
Of centuries breaks, cracks, begins to move.
The thunder is the thunder of the floes,
The thaw, the flood, the upstart Spring.

Thank God our time is now when wrong
Comes up to face us everywhere,
Never to leave us till we take
The longest stride of soul men ever took.

Affairs are now soul size.
The enterprise
Is exploration into God,
Where no nation's foot has ever trodden yet.

Why Jesus? What is my response to the challenge of a Savior who comes with the power of God yet works through the weakness of men? Am I willing to work with Him and for Him, to suffer with Him and endure all that He endures until my own heart is purified like gold in the furnace? Can I accept a God who saves me, not by breaking the strength of my temptations or my enemies, but by summoning me to endure and to overcome them? Not by substituting His miracles for my incompetence, but by requiring me to use my human powers in a way that is divine? If so, then I can accept the mystery of the Messiah whose mission is to be the "Suffering Servant."

But this is not all Jesus is. He is also the *Anointed of God*. His weakness is stronger than the power of men; His very defeat is His victory (see 1 *Corinthians* 1:18 ff.). And Matthew takes care in the very beginning of his Gospel to assure us that in the end it is Jesus who triumphs.

After Herod's death, he tells us, "the angel of the Lord appeared in a dream to Joseph in Egypt with the command: "Get up, take the child and his mother, and set out for the land of Israel. Those who had designs on the life of the child are dead" (*Matthew* 2:19-20).

Joseph did as he was told. But because Herod's son was reigning in Judea he was afraid to go back to Bethlehem. Instead he went to the region of Galilee. There he settled in a town called Nazareth. And, Matthew tells us, "In this way what was said through the prophet was fulfilled: 'He shall be called a Nazorean'" (*Matthew* 2:19-23).

Christ's return to Nazareth is a preview of His triumphant return to earth at the end of time. In spite of the fact that Jesus is left in weakness and His enemies in power, every effort of Herod to destroy Him fails. And so will every effort of Christ's enemies to destroy Him fail until the end of time. In fact, the opposition of His enemies becomes the very means through which God's own redemptive plans and prophecies are fulfilled, as Matthew pointed out earlier in connection with the flight into Egypt (see verse 15: "Out of Egypt I have called my son") and now points out about his return to Nazareth (verse 23: "He shall be called a Nazorean"). Already we have here a foreshadowing of Christ's simultaneous defeat and victory on the cross.

Matthew emphasizes the fact of Herod's death (see verses 15, 19, 20). This suggests that Matthew is telling us more than just a fact; he is making a statement of principle as well: "Those who had designs on the life of the child are dead." Jesus *is* life. Apart from Him no one can live (see *John* 14:6; 15:4-6). All those who oppose Him are in the way of death and are in reality dead already no matter how strong or powerful they may appear to be.

Through Him all things came into being,
and apart from him nothing came to be.

Whatever came to be in him found life,
life for the light of men. (*John* 1:3-4)

We ask again the question, "Why Jesus?" The answer is, "Because He is victory. He wins. He is the Anointed of God."

Here the point is only hinted at and suggested. But throughout the Gospel it will be made with increasing insistence (see *Matthew* 8:18-34; 10:26-42; 16:24-28). Finally, when Jesus is brought to trial before the Sanhedrin (*Matthew* 26:57-68) it is made most forcefully of all.

The full impact of Jesus' words before the Sanhedrin could be lost on us unless we put ourselves into the mind-set of Jesus' contemporaries. The one thing every Jew of Jesus' time took for granted about the Messiah was that he could not be, would not be, defeated by his enemies. To be victorious over one's enemies was one of the surest signs of God's favor, and it was to be expected of the Messiah, God's chosen one, His Anointed, more than of anyone else. The Psalmist sang: "That you love me I know by this, that my enemy does not triumph over me" (*Psalms*

41:12), and this was the experience of the great prophets (see 1 *Kings*, chapter 18 and *Jeremiah* 20:11 for example). It is true that the defeat of the just by the wicked was recognized as not necessarily being the last word (see *Wisdom*, chapters 2 and 3; *Psalms* 49). But the defeat of the Messiah, who was sent precisely to overcome God's enemies, was unthinkable.

Yet Jesus stood before the Sanhedrin defeated.

It was in this context, when Jesus had been deserted by His friends, captured by His enemies, bound, beaten and delivered up to the Sanhedrin for judgment, and obviously abandoned by God, that the high priest rose and called on Jesus to answer: "I order you to tell us under oath before the living God whether you are the Messiah, the Son of God."

Even to Jesus it was obvious He was not — at least according to everything He had been brought up as a Jew to believe. How could He claim to be the favored, the chosen, the Anointed One of God when every sign of God's favor and protection was taken away from Him? If *God* wasn't saying that He was the chosen one, what right had Jesus to say it? On what could He base His claim?

And yet He did say it. He quoted the prophecy of Daniel who saw:

> One like a son of man coming,
>   on the clouds of heaven;
> When he reached the Ancient One
>   and was presented before him,
> He received dominion, glory, and kingship;
>   nations and peoples of every language serve him.
> His dominion is an everlasting dominion
>   that shall not be taken away,
>   his kingship shall not be destroyed.
> (*Daniel* 7:13-14)

This was a prophecy about the Messiah. It echoed the prophecy of Nathan about the promised "Son of David" (2 *Samuel* 7:8-16). In applying it to Himself, Jesus left no doubt about the fact that He was claiming, even in those circumstances of apparently total abandonment by God, to be the chosen Messiah.

On what could He base such a claim?

There could only be one explanation. If Jesus still believed He was the Messiah when every sign of God's favor was withdrawn from Him, then this could only mean one thing: that He was claiming to be the Messiah by *nature*.

He was saying, "I need no sign that God has chosen me. I cannot *not* be the Messiah. I am the Messiah by nature. *I AM!*"

This was a claim to be God Himself (see *Exodus* 3:14; *John* 8:58). The high priest recognized it at once and denounced it as blasphemy (*Matthew* 26:65). On these grounds Jesus was condemned.

Our faith in Jesus must be as absolute as this. We must believe in His presence, His power, His victory over sin and death, and in His present, saving, redemptive action in our lives even when there is no sign of it at all. Not only that, but we are called to *persevere* in this belief no matter how victorious Christ's enemies may appear to be, no matter how weak or absent God may seem to be.

Our faith in the *will* and the *power* of Jesus to triumph over all the destructive forces in the world (and in our own selves) must depend on nothing except our absolute knowledge of *who He is*. It must not depend on signs, wonders, or any evidence at all that He is in fact being victorious on earth. It must not go up and down with the apparent success or failure of His mission, or of the work of His people, the Church. We do not believe Jesus is God because He is victorious; we believe He is and will be victorious because He is God — because He cannot *not* be. Jesus is God. And therefore He is life and victory and salvation. "His dominion is an everlasting dominion that shall not be taken away. His kingship shall not be destroyed" (*Daniel* 7:14).

This is the message of the book of Revelation, which was written to provide a pattern for Christian thinking during times of persecution. In the midst of every calamity and disaster, when the world is falling around us and persecution is raging unchecked, the book of Revelation tells us what our Christian attitude should be. It is echoed in the hymns that punctuate the book:

"Holy, holy, holy is the Lord
  God Almighty,
He who was, and who is, and
  who is to come. . .

"With your blood you purchased
  for God
men of every race and nation.
You made of them a kingdom,
and priests to serve our God,
and they shall reign on the earth. . .

"To the One seated on the
  throne, and to the Lamb,
be praise, and honor, glory and
  might,
forever and ever!"

(Revelation 4:8; 5:9-13. See also 3:7; 4:12; 7:15; 11:16; 12:10; 15:3; 16:5 and chapters 19-22)

Why Jesus? Simply because He is by nature the Way, the Truth and the Life (*John* 14:6). He cannot

*not* be this. There is no just and saving God but Him
(*Isaiah* 45:21). Jesus is the keystone of the arch, the
cornerstone of the building, the foundation of life
itself. "There is no salvation in anyone else, for there
is no other name in the whole world given to men by
which we are to be saved" (*Acts* 4:11-12; see also
1 *Corinthians* 3:11; *Matthew* 21:42; *John* 6:66-49).

Jesus Himself answered the question "Why Jesus?" in the last lines of Matthew's Gospel:

> "Full authority has been given to me
> both in heaven and on earth;
> go, therefore, and make disciples of
> all the nations. . .
> And know that I am with you always,
> until the end of the world!" (*Matthew* 28:18-20)

This was Jesus' final revelation of Himself as the
promised "Son of David". With these words Matthew
ends his Gospel on the same note that began it: "a
record of Jesus Christ, Son of David. . ." (see
*Matthew* 1:1).

Why Jesus?

Because He is the Anointed One of God.

### CHAPTER ELEVEN: JESUS IS VICTORY
*Matthew* 2:19-23

*Summary:*

1. Jesus triumphs over all opposition and efforts to destroy
   Him. Though the second Herod, like the first, tries to "exile"
   Him from earth through crucifixion, Jesus will return victorious "on the clouds of heaven" (*Matthew* 26:64) even as
   He returned safe to Nazareth. He is not simply a man
   involved in a struggle with evil; He is the Anointed Son of
   God. He is life, and all who oppose Him are "dead" by that
   very fact.
2. Our faith in the victory of Christ must be absolute. We must
   believe in His will and power to triumph over sin and evil,
   both in ourselves and in the world, regardless of how

discouraging the visible situation may be. Our trust in Christ's victory must be founded on His identity as the Anointed Son of God. It cannot depend on signs, wonders, or visible evidence of His power.

3. Our faith must be characterized by perseverance. It must be an echoing response to God's "enduring love" (see *John* 1:14, 17; *Exodus* 34:6). Our faith in Christ risen, triumphant, and coming again on the "clouds of heaven" is expressed in persevering fidelity, especially in the face of discouragement, defeat and persecution.

4. Christian life in the world is an active waiting — in faith and fidelity — for Christ to come again. Fidelity is faith carried out into action. Our faith is expressed in undiscouraged, unremitting efforts to establish the kingship of Christ over all creation, in every area and activity of human life.

*Questions for prayer and discussion:*

1. Do I believe that Christ is stronger than all the forces of evil presently at work in the world? Where do I encounter the power of evil in my own life and work? In my family life? In my social life? In my business or profession? How do I show in action that I believe Jesus is stronger than the power of evil which I meet in these situations?

2. Do my confidence and my enthusiasm as a Christian rise and fall according to the signs that Christ is winning? Do I write off any individuals, any movements, any areas of human activity as hopelessly under the power of evil? Of ignorance, illusion, or apathy?

3. Does my respect for the Church go up and down according to the evidence that she is succeeding in her mission? Do I believe in the Church because she is helping people, or do I believe she is helping people because she is the Church? Am I as devoted to the weak and failing humanity of Christ on earth today as I am to Christ inspiring and triumphant?

4. This chapter invites me to unconditional perseverance in faith and fidelity; that is, to commit myself until death to *believe* in the victory of Christ and to *work* to bring it to actualization in every area and activity of human life. Am I ready to make this commitment? Why?

## CHAPTER TWELVE

## JESUS IS SAVIOR IN ACTION

After recounting the return of Jesus to Nazareth, Matthew skips some twenty-five or thirty years and takes up his narrative again with the preaching of John the Baptizer (chapter 3:1).

This is a change of theme. The emphasis now is less on *announcing* the event of the Messiah's coming into this world and more on a *call to discipleship.* Once we know that the Anointed One has come, and that He is the "saving presence of God on earth," what do we do about it?

John the Baptizer says, "Reform your lives." Change your minds about attitudes and values; change the goal toward which your behavior is directed. Follow Jesus as the "Master of the Way." Be His disciples.

This gives us another answer to our question, "Why Jesus? Why should I base my life on relationship with Him?"

The answer is, "Because He is the Master of the Way. He is a teacher, *the* Teacher of Life. Through conversion to Christ (*Matthew* 3:1-12) we are brought into the experience of God and of our relatedness with Him (3:13-17). From Jesus we learn

what is the authentic way of God, and what is the
deception of the devil (4:1-11). Jesus is light in the
darkness of the world (4:12-16). He invites us to come
apart with Him (v. 12) and open ourselves up to His
light. Then Jesus Himself calls us to conversion
(4:17-22).

Discipleship is not the theme of this book, and so
we will not try here to develop Matthew's presenta-
tion of Jesus as the "Master of the Way." That is for a
later book, which will include the Sermon on the
Mount (*Matthew*, chapters 5-7), in which Matthew
shows us Jesus the Teacher in action.

Just before the Sermon on the Mount, however,
Matthew inserts a striking sentence into his Gospel.
At least it becomes striking when we find the same
sentence repeated, almost word-for-word, five chapters later. The sentence reads:

> Jesus toured all of Galilee. He taught in their syna-
> gogues, proclaimed the good news of the kingdom,
> and cured the people of every disease and illness
> (chapter 4:23).

This sentence, with the paragraph that follows it, is
the last thing Matthew writes before introducing the
long discourse or monologue section which we call
the Sermon on the Mount.[1] It seems all the more
significant, therefore, to find the same sentence repeated word-for-word just before the *next* long discourse section in Matthew, which is made up of
instructions Christ gave His twelve apostles before
sending them out on mission (chapter ten). The
second time the sentence reads:

> Jesus continued his tour of all the towns and villages.
> He taught in their synagogues, he proclaimed the
> good news of God's reign, and he cured every sickness
> and disease (chapter 9:35).[2]

We have already pointed out (chapter two above) that biblical manuscripts didn't have chapter headings and subtitles to indicate a change of theme, or to block off sections of material into units. The writer had to do that by inserting clues into the text itself. And a sentence repeated word-for-word is liable to be such a clue. The two identical sentences may serve as brackets to indicate the beginning and the end of a particular block of matter.

It is logical to see these two sentences as doing just that. Matthew has just finished introducing Jesus as Savior and Teacher: as the "saving presence of God on earth," and as "Master of the Way." He has shown Jesus beginning His missionary work and calling others to follow Him. Now he blocks off between these two identical sentences a long section which includes:

1. the Sermon on the Mount (chapters 5-7)
2. Jesus' first missionary tour (chapters 8-9)

It is reasonable enough to suppose that Matthew intends in these four chapters to show us *Jesus in action*, first as teacher and "Master of the Way" (the Sermon on the Mount, chapters 5-7); then as missionary, healer and "saving presence of God on earth" (chapters 8-9).

We could say, then, that the first nine chapters of Matthew's Gospel deal with two things: *evangelization*, or the call to accept Jesus as Savior and Lord; and *discipleship*, or the call to learn from Him as teacher and "Master of the Way." Jesus is announced as the saving presence of God on earth in chapters one and two, and shown being this in action in chapters eight and nine. He is announced as teacher of life or "Master of the Way" in chapters three and four, and shown being this in action in chapters five and seven (the Sermon on the Mount). This, at least, is the outline we have chosen to follow in this book.

But since this book does not deal with discipleship or with Jesus as "Master of the Way," we will skip the Sermon on the Mount and go directly to chapters eight and nine.

These chapters are introduced (together with the Sermon on the Mount) by the sentence we have quoted: "Jesus *toured* all of Galilee. He *taught* in their synagogues, *proclaimed* the good news of the kingdom, and *cured* the people of every disease and illness."

As the saving presence of God on earth He toured; He made Himself present to His people where they were, in all the towns and villages. As *Emmanuel* — "God with us" — He made it possible for us to enter into personal relationship and friendship with God, and to interact with Him in concrete, human ways.

As light of the world and "Master of the Way" He taught. He changed the Law of the Ten Commandments into a way of perfection in grace. He expressed the truth of God in human words and made it possible for us to come to know the mind and heart of God through His words.

As the long-awaited Messiah He proclaimed the good news of His coming, and of the reign of God which His coming inaugurated: the fulfillment of the promises; the overcoming of sin and darkness and death; a new meaning and purpose in existence; the sharing of God's life with men, and the reconciliation of all creation "in Christ."

As the Anointed Savior and Lord He cured. He cured the body of illness and the soul of sin. "They carried to him all those afflicted with various diseases and racked with pain: the possessed, the lunatics, the paralyzed. He cured them all" (*Matthew* 4:24). He showed Himself to be, not only the Savior, but the saving *destiny* of all mankind. True healing is in the surrender of all we are to Him; and total healing is to enter totally into that fullness of life which is found in union with Him who is not only the way and the truth but life itself (*John* 14:6).

And this is the ministry of Jesus.

In this first missionary tour Matthew shows us Jesus being in action all that it was announced in the first chapters of the Gospel that He would be. These stories give us an opportunity to contemplate Jesus relating to a variety of different people in a variety of ways, according to the different titles and roles that describe His saving relationship to the human race and to each individual one of us. When we ask the question, "Why Jesus? How do I need Him? What might He mean to me?" we can look for an answer by asking which one of the encounters with Jesus described in these chapters we relate to most affectively. What action, what words of Jesus move me most deeply in these chapters? What seems to address most my own relationship — or need of relationship — with Him? What title describes best the Jesus who answers the desire of my own heart?

The first title Matthew gives to Jesus in his Gospel is "Son of David." This is, in fact, the theme of his Gospel (see *Matthew* 1:1-17 and chapter two above). And this theme runs throughout all the incidents Matthew presents for our consideration in this section of his Gospel that we are looking at now. In everything Jesus says and does in these two chapters, He displays the power and authority of the promised "Son of David" (see for example, 7:28-29; 8:8-9; 8:27; 8:29; 9:6-8).

He shows His authority over:

— *sickness* by curing it (see 8:1-17)
— *people* by the demands He makes on their un-limited devotion (see 8:18-22)
— *nature* by calming the wind and the storm (see 8:23-27)
— *demons* by expelling them (see 8:28-34)
— *sin* by forgiving it (see 9:1-8)
— *the law* by reinterpreting it (see 9:9-13)
— *devotional practices* (e.g., fasting) by making Himself their object! (see 9:14-17)
— *death itself* by recalling a little girl to life (see 9:18-26)

And the section ends with the cure of two blind men who call out to Him directly, using the title "Son of David" (see 9:27-31).[3]

"Son of David" is a theme, then, which runs through all the narrative section of chapters eight and nine. But in the particular events of these chapters, the power and authority which belong to Jesus as Son of David are shown used in a way that brings out His other titles also.

*Jesus-Emmanuel*:

The first concrete revelation of this power and authority is given in the cure of the leper (ch. 8:1-4). In this story and in the other healing miracles that fol-low it — the cure of the centurion's servant, of Peter's mother-in-law, and of all the afflicted and possessed they brought to him that same evening (8:5-16) — we see Jesus living up to the name that Joseph was told to give him, the name that means "God saves"; "You are to name him Jesus because he will save his people from their sins" (*Matthew* 1:21). Jesus is the Savior, the healing, saving presence of God on earth. He goes out in universal, saving love to all men: to the *outcasts* (the leper: 8:1-4); to the *pagans* (the centurion: 8:5-13); and to the ordinary people (8:14-17). And he heals as *Emmanuel*, God present and walking among us (see 8:15, for example: "He took her by the hand. . .").

### Universal Lord

This saving mission of Jesus is extended to all men because Jesus is the Lord of all. Matthew has already shown us in the story of the astrologers (2:1-12) that Jesus is the universal Lord and destiny of every man and woman born into this world. Now, in the cure of the Roman centurion's servant (8:5-13) he shows us again how the Father draws not only Jews but pagans to His Son. Jesus Himself is amazed (8:10) at the faith of the centurion, a faith evoked in him, not by the word of God in Scripture, since he was ignorant of the Scriptures, but by whatever "star" the Father drew him by.

In the story of the centurion Jesus also appears again as the "crisis" and judgment of every human life (see chapter eight above). In the centurion, as in the astrologers, the pagan world responds to Jesus with faith while many of His own people, like Herod, are rejecting Him. Simeon had prophesied, "This child is destined to be the downfall and the rise of many in Israel, a sign that will be opposed . . . so that the thoughts of many hearts may be laid bare" (*Luke* 2:34). Jesus echoes this prophecy in His response to the centurion as He exclaims: "Mark what I say! Many will come from the east (cp. *Matthew* 2:1) and the west and will find a place at the banquet in the kingdom of God with Abraham, Issac, and Jacob, while the natural heirs of the kingdom will be driven out into the dark" (*Matthew* 8:11-12). Every human being, no matter what his or her race, nationality or culture may be, sooner or later encounters Jesus Christ. And each one's response to that encounter is his "judgment."

## The "Suffering Servant"

At the end of this first round of healing miracles Matthew inserts by way of commentary a verse from Isaiah that doesn't seem to fit. Jesus expelled evil spirits by a simple command, Matthew tells us, and cured all who were afflicted, "thereby fulfilling what had been said through Isaiah the prophet:

'It was our infirmities he bore, our sufferings he endured'" (*Matthew* 8:16-17).

This citation from Isaiah doesn't seem to apply. Jesus is curing by a "simple command." He has not yet borne our infirmities or our sufferings. That side of His redemptive ministry will not appear until He begins to predict His passion in chapter sixteen. Still, Matthew refers to it here.

He is already making the point, as he made it in the second chapter of his Gospel (2:13-18), that Jesus is the "Suffering Servant." He is a Savior who saves through weakness and defeat. And all who follow Him must expect to endure with Him the hardship of their own weakness multiplied by the persecution of His enemies.

This is the paradox of salvation: that it is precisely through the experience of weakness, deprivation and defeat that we are brought by God to the fullness of life. Jesus Himself was made perfect through suffering (*Hebrews* 2:10; 4:5; 5:7-9), and He heals us, paradoxically, by joining us to Himself in

His own endurance of the sin and hostility of the world. He saves us by being, both for us and within us, the "Suffering Servant."

The mystery of Christ's redemptive role as suffering Savior is deeper than this, of course. He is the "Lamb of God" who takes away — by taking upon Himself — the sins of the world. But Matthew is not yet introducing us to that mystery, and we will not enter into it here. It is enough for us at this point to see how Jesus, by being the "Suffering Servant" who calls us to endure with Him instead of making everything easy for us, is a Savior who summons us to grow. He doesn't just "rescue" us like inert, unconscious victims. He truly *saves* our human existence in this world by calling and empowering us to live our human lives on the level of God's own divine operation.

And so we see Jesus in this section of the Gospel challenging those who would follow Him to go beyond their human level of attitudes, values and behavior. To the scribe who says, "Teacher, wherever you go I will come after you," Jesus answers, "The foxes have lairs, the birds in the sky have nests, but the Son of Man has nowhere to lay his head." He tells another who wants to fulfill his social obligations to his family first by an appropriate period of mourning for his deceased father, "Follow me, and let the dead bury their dead" (8:19-21).

Jesus challenges us to put our trust in something beyond the security of home and possessions and to live by pure, supernatural hope in God (see *Matthew* 6:19-34; 7:24-27). He calls us to break with cultural patterns and values in order to walk by the new light of God in supernatural faith (see *Romans* 12:2, *John* 15:18-19 and 17:9-19; 1 *Peter* 2:9-17). And He teaches us to love one another, no longer just by the natural, even instinctive bonds of family and relationship but by that supernatural love poured out in our hearts through the Holy Spirit which unites us to God as our Father and to the rest of the redeemed as our brothers and sisters in Christ (see *Luke* 14:26; *Matthew* 12: 47-50 and 23:9; *Romans* 5:5). Where there is pain in following Jesus, it is mostly the pain of growth in supernatural faith, hope and love. We resist God interiorly only in the measure that we resist the fullness of life.

### *The Anointed One*

Jesus can ask all of us because He gives All. He can ask us to give up every security on earth because He is security itself. He is not just the "Suffering Servant" — He is the Anointed and Lord.

The point is made in the next event Matthew reports: the storm on the lake (8:23-27). After warning the scribe who would follow Him that He has no home, no safe place to lay His Head, Jesus sets out across unpredictable Lake Gennesaret (the Sea of Galilee) in a small boat with His apostles. A storm comes up and the boat is being swamped by the waves. A less secure situation could hardly be imagined. But Jesus is sleeping soundly in the boat. When the desciples awaken Him, He stands up and rebukes the winds and the sea. And complete calm follows.

Jesus triumphs. He is Lord. He may live and work in weakness, and leave His followers subject to the winds and the storms of persecution and of every other disaster. But He is in control. He is Lord.

In his second chapter, when he told about Jesus' return to Nazareth, Matthew seemed to be making the point that Jesus *is* life, and that all who oppose Him are already dead, or in the way of death, just by that fact (see 2:20). Now, in this chapter he seems to be saying the same thing, but by contrasting the security and comfort of "home" with the danger and hardship, the insecurity and exposure, of travel. To be with Jesus is to have no place to lay one's head; it is to be on the open sea, on the lonely road. But to be with Jesus is to be safe, because Jesus is security itself. Even in a leaky rowboat in the middle of a lake during a storm one is safe if Jesus is there. And if Jesus is not there, no one is safe, not even in the security of one's own home.

We find this idea emphasized in the next event Matthew recounts. Jesus is travelling still, in an area that is unsafe for travel because two men possessed by demons live there, making their home in some tombs close to the road. They were "so savage that no one could travel along that road."

We have here the twin sources of man's insecurity: sin and death. Those who threatened the road were "possessed by demons" and they were "coming out of the tombs." Jesus shows His power over both sin and death by casting out the demons and letting the men go free. The demons ask, however, to enter a herd of swine instead; and when they do the whole herd goes rushing down the bluff into the sea and is drowned (*Matthew* 8:28-32).

With Jesus the disciples escaped drowning in the middle of the sea during a storm. Apart from Jesus these pigs managed to drown while peacefully grazing on the high, safe ground of their own pasture! Security is not in where you are; it is in whom you are with. Jesus will say it later: "He who is not with me is against me, and he who does not gather with me scatters" (*Matthew* 12:30).

Once again Matthew has made his point: Jesus is the Anointed Son of God. He is Lord. He redeems us

through suffering and weakness, but He triumphs
with the power of God. He *is* the way, the truth and
the life.

## *Conclusion*

In the events of Christ's first missionary tour that
he narrates in this chapter, Matthew shows us Jesus
being in action all that was announced of Him. This
chapter invites us to contemplate Jesus in these different moments of encounter with other human beings — to put ourselves in imagination into the scenes
Matthew describes — and to see how we ourselves
best relate to Him.

What is Jesus for me? He is all that is described
here, of course, but what is He mostly and above all
for me right now? Do I relate to Him most affectively,
most deeply at this moment in my life as healer and
Savior — just as *Jesus*: "God saves"? Or do I relate to
Him most as *Emmanuel*: God present among us, God
drawn humanly close?

Have I encountered Jesus as universal Lord? As
answering a desire and a call so deep in my being, so
directly from God Himself, that I have never even
been able to identify it? Am I aware that, precisely
because of this fact (because He responds to the very
core experience of my existence, to my deepest, in-
articulate consciousness of who and what I am) Jesus
is the "crisis" of my life? Am I aware that the whole
orientation of my being hinges on the response I make
to Him? And is this the point at which I find myself
right now in acting out the drama of my life?

Or do I relate most to Jesus now as "Suffering
Servant"? As the one who challenges my orbit, who
calls me off the established plane of my existence? Do
I find Him allowing me to experience with Him the
questions of life that only faith can answer? Is He

leading me through the experience of insecurity, fragility and weakness to trust absolutely in the Father? Is He calling me, not away from, but *beyond* every relationship of love in my life to adore God as the One who alone is my All? And do I find in the very pain of going higher, a deeper, more piercing awareness of the fullness of supernatural life?

Or do I need most of all to focus on Jesus as the Anointed One, the Son of God who triumphs because He cannot *not* triumph, and whose victory, however inapparent, is assured? Is *perseverance* the fulcrum of my spiritual life at this time, so that the responses I make to God and to other in the present are but the expression of my abiding expectation of the future? Is my prayer "Maranatha! Come, Lord Jesus!" (see 1 *Corinthians* 16:22; *Revelation* 22:20)? Is the Jesus I cry out to the "Alpha and the Omega, the First and the Last, the Beginning and the End," the victorious Savior who was, who is, and who is yet to come? (see *Revelation* 22:12 ff.).

Who is Jesus? What is He for me? Why Jesus? Why Jesus for me right now?

### FOOTNOTES

[1] A significant feature of Matthew's Gospel, which most Scripture scholars use as the basis for their study outline, are the five discourse or sermon sections — each alternating with a narrative section — which end with the identical phrase "And it happened that when Jesus had finished. . ." (see 7:28; 11:1; 13:53; 19:1; 26:1). The first of these is the Sermon on the Mount.

[2] In Greek the two texts are even more identical than they appear here. The English translator used different words — synonyms — to translate some words in the second sentence which in Greek are identically the same as in the first sentence. It makes no difference, since the meaning is exactly the same and the parallelism just as obvious.

[3] There are only three places in Matthew's Gospel where Jesus is directly addressed as "Son of David." They are 9:27, 15:22 and 20:30. Other uses of the title are not in direct address (for

example, 12:23 and 21:9). I think it is legitimate to presume that these three verses signal a change of theme each time they appear, and that Matthew's Gospel can be reflected on as inviting us to four significant responses: first, to accept *Jesus* as the saving light and life of God on earth (*Matthew* 1-9); secondly, to accept the *Church* as the continuation of His incarnate presence on earth (*Matthew* 10 to 16:12); thirdly, to accept *life in the Church* as a dying to self and to all things in order to live totally for God and other people in love (*Matthew* 16:13 to the end of ch. 20); and fourthly, to accept *Christian life in the world* as a persevering in faith and fidelity until Christ comes again (*Matthew* 21-28). The invocations, "Son of David, have pity. . ." alert us to the change of theme each time.

## CHAPTER TWELVE: JESUS IS SAVIOR IN ACTION —
### *Matthew*, chapter eight

*Summary:*

1. Chapter eight of Matthew's Gospel shows Jesus being in action what it was announced in chapters one and two He would be: "the saving presence of God on earth," touring, teaching, proclaiming the good news and curing with the power and authority of the promised "Son of David."

2. In the first healing miracles of this chapter (8:1-16) we see Jesus revealed as "*Jesus-Emmanuel*," God present among us to save us, God healing us by His presence, His touch, by personal, human contact.

3. With the cure of the Roman centurion's servant (8:5-13), Jesus is shown reaching out to the pagan world as *universal Lord*. The centurion's faith, contrasted with the rejection Christ experienced from His own people, reveals Him again as the "crisis" — the judgment — of every human existence.

4. Matthew tells us, anachronistically, that Jesus heals by taking our sufferings on Himself (8:17). This and the challenge Jesus holds up to those who would follow him (8:18-22) reveal Him as the "*Suffering Servant*" who calls us beyond human life to share in the life and activity of God.

5. When Jesus calms the storm on the lake (8:23-27) and expels the demons from the men who made the road unsafe to travel in Gadara (8:28-34), He reveals Himself as the *Anointed Son of God*, who triumphs because He cannot *not* triumph. Jesus *is* life; He *is* security. To be with Him is to be secure in the "way, the truth and the life," simply because Jesus is God.

*Questions for prayer and discussion:*

1. Which one of these stories calls forth the most affective response from me? Why? How do I relate most easily to Jesus? Is this the way I relate to Him habitually in my prayer?

2. Does any of these stories upset me or disturb me? How do I respond to that? Do I find here something about Jesus I am misunderstanding? Something I really do not accept?

3. Do these titles of Jesus mean more to me now: "Jesus," "Emmanuel," "Universal Lord and destiny," "Suffering Servant," "Anointed Son of God"? Can I "breathe" them from the heart with the Holy Spirit the way the Father "breathes forth" the name of His Son? Can I speak them affectively, with intimate knowledge and love, conscious as I do so that I am sharing with the Father in uttering the Word that He has spoken from all eternity?

4. This chapter is an invitation to *contemplate* Jesus in action; that is, to see Him, and be with Him in imagination, watching Him, listening to Him, responding to Him in my imagination in whatever way is natural for me. Have I ever tried this form of prayer? Do I intend to try it? Why?

## CHAPTER THIRTEEN

## JESUS IS TEACHER OF LIFE

It is difficult — and not true to reality — to separate Jesus as Savior and healer — the saving presence of God on earth — from Jesus the teacher and "Master of the Way." He is the one by being the other. St. John was so aware of this that he made the identification of the two roles a theme of his Gospel: Jesus is "light and life" interchangeably. He is the "light of life" (*John* 8:12); and the life that He is is light:

> Whatever came to be in him,
>    found life,
> life for the light of men.

> Eternal life is this:
> to *know you*, the only true
>    God,
> and him whom you have sent,
>    Jesus Christ. (*John* 1:4 and 17:3)

We have said above, however, that Matthew in his Gospel presents Jesus first as Savior and healer (*Matthew* 1-2) then as teacher (*Matthew* 3-4), and that the Sermon on the Mount (*Matthew* 5-7) shows Jesus the Teacher in action, while the two narrative chapters that follow the Sermon (*Matthew* 8-9) show

Him on His first missionary tour as Savior and healer. It would probably be more precise to say that chapter eight of Matthew's Gospel shows Jesus being in action the Savior that it was announced He would be in Matthew's first two chapters — shows Him, that is, as Son of David, Jesus-Emmanuel, Universal Lord and destiny of all men, the "Suffering Servant," and the Anointed Son of God — while chapter nine shows Jesus being in action what was announced of Him in chapters three and four.

In these chapters (three and four) Jesus begins already to appear as the Teacher, the "Master of the Way." He calls us, through the preaching of John the Baptizer, to conversion (3:1-12). He offers us, through this conversion, the experience of God and of our own relatedness to the Father — even as He experienced His relatedness to the Father at the moment of His symbolic gesture of conversion, His baptism in the Jordan (3:13-17). Jesus shows us during His temptations in the desert how to see through the deceits of the devil (4:1-11). He calls us apart with Himself to enlighten our hearts (4:12-16), and then He Himself begins to call to conversion and to a higher, transcendent purpose of life (4:17-22).

In all of these events Jesus is announced to us as one who saves by teaching us the way, by sharing with us His truth, by being for us the light that is life. He is the way, the truth and the life.

And now in chapter nine of Matthew's Gospel we find Jesus on His first missionary tour doing all of these things in action.

### Call to conversion

The theme of conversion is already introduced at the end of chapter eight, when the people of Gadara (where Jesus drove the demons out of the possessed

men and into the pigs) have to make a choice: Shall
they invite Jesus to stay in their territory and risk
some more unexpected happenings — such as, perhaps, the loss of more pigs — or shall they politely ask
Him to leave?

The townsfolk of Gadara opt for life as they have
grown used to it. They would prefer that Jesus left the
demons in their possessed fellow citizens and their
pigs in the pasture! They beg Him to leave their
neighborhood. So Jesus gets into the boat and crosses
back over the lake to His "own town" of Capernaum
(8:33-9:1).

When Jesus arrives in Capernaum they bring
Him a paralyzed man lying on a mat (see *Matthew*
9:1-8). Instead of curing the man's paralysis, which is
what they obviously desired, Jesus addresses his
heart. He calls him to an interior conversion, to a
healing of his sins: "Have courage, son, your sins are
forgiven." Then, to prove He has the authority to
forgive sins He tells the paralyzed man to stand up
and walk.

John baptized with water. He predicted, though,
that the one coming after him would baptize "in the
Holy Spirit and fire" (3:11). Jesus does not just
summon us to repentance; He gives us the power to
rise up from the paralyzing death of sin and to walk in
the new way of life. This is the gift of the Spirit (see 3
*John* 1:2-4; 2 *Corinthians* 12:18).

The paralyzed man had to make a choice. He had
to decide whether or not to believe in Jesus' words
and to act on them. There was no cure until he acted
(cp. 3:8: "Give some evidence that you mean to
reform"). When he made his decision and stood up,
he found he was able to walk.

And this was his experience of God. It was also

the experience of the bystanders: "At the sight, a feeling of awe came over the crowd, and they praised God for giving such authority to men" (9:8).

## The "temptations"

During his temptations in the desert (*Matthew* 4:1-11) Jesus appeared as "Master of the Way" by unmasking the deceits of the devil. Now in chapter nine we find Him doing the same thing, but this time in response to the illusions and misconceptions of men.

Jesus calls a tax-collector named Matthew to follow Him (*Matthew* 9:9-13). Actually, the man's name was Levi — see *Mark* 2:14 — but he changed it later). This was not what the Messiah was supposed to do. First of all, Matthew did not keep the Jewish law (9:11), and the Messiah, as a good Jew and upholder of the Law, was expected to purge the land of such people. Secondly, as a tax collector Matthew worked for the Romans and was considered a traitor. The Messiah was supposed to overcome the Romans and restore the political supremacy of Israel. Jesus should have treated Matthew as an enemy. And finally, the Messiah was expected to bring prosperity to the people (cp. Christ's first temptation in the desert: "If you are the Son of God, command these stones to turn into bread"). But Matthew, by gouging unjust taxes out of poor fishermen, was taking the bread from their mouths.

Jesus should have indicted him, not invited him.

But He just said, "Follow me." And worse yet, when Matthew invited Jesus to eat with him and his tax-collector friends, Jesus went. This was a scandal to the Pharisees, who asked his disciples, "What reason can the Teacher have for eating with tax collectors and those who disregard the law?"

They had their answer in the question itself: the reason was that Jesus *was* the Teacher, the "Master of the Way." He had come to reveal the true meaning of salvation, to show what the real mission and goal of the Messiah was. It was not to give prosperity and power to His people on this earth; it was to call them to fullness of life — that is, to participation in the divine life of God (cp. *Matthew* 4:4; "Not on bread alone is man to live, but on every utterance that comes from the mouth of God"). Jesus came, not to overpower the sinners and the traitors but to convert them; to call them into unity with Himself and give them a new kind of nourishment in the "breaking of the bread." His banquet with the tax collectors and sinners at Matthew's house was already a preview and a revelation, for those who had eyes to see, of what His mission as Messiah was. Christ's answer to the scandal of the Pharisees was to call them — and us along with them — to supernatural *faith* in the true goal of His mission.

### The question of fasting

A second "temptation" of Christ occurs in this section when some of John the Baptizer's disciples ask Jesus why His disciples don't fast (*Matthew* 9:14-17).

The presumption of John's disciples was that getting holy is essentially a matter of doing the right things. Religious people prayed; they fasted; they gave alms. These practices, and others like them, went with being holy like exercise goes with being an athlete. How could the disciples of Jesus, then, be holy if they didn't follow the get-holy regime?

Jesus enlightens them as Teacher of the Way by correcting their misconceptions about two things: first, about what the holiness He came to give consists in; secondly, about the means to achieve it.

Christian holiness is not a matter of what we do; it is a matter of what we become. To be holy means for a Christian to be identified with Christ. It means to be one with Him as the members of a body are one with the head. To be holy is to share the life of God who alone is truly holy (see *Matthew* 19:17); and this life is shared with us "in Christ" (see above, chapters two and four). Holiness is not a matter of achieving a certain level of human behavior. It isn't essentially performance. It is union — union with God. Jesus will compare this later to the union of the branches with the vine (*John* 15:1 ff.). Paul uses the image of the body and its members (*Romans* 12:4-5; 1 *Corinthians*, ch. 12). But at this point the image of union Jesus uses is that of the bride and the bridegroom (*Matthew* 9:15). This is a union of mind and heart and will with God, and it is the goal and the fruit of grace.[1]

If we are truly one with God in a union of shared life with Him (which is grace) we will act on His level, of course (see *Colossians* 4:1-11; 1 *Corinthians* 6: 15-20; 1 *John* 3:9-10). But that is not a level it is in our power to achieve. All the fasting, prayer and almsgiving in the world are not enough, in themselves, to bring us there.

We must be made new. To be one with Christ through grace is to be a "new creation" (2 *Corinthians* 6:17). It is to "lay aside" one's "old self which deteriorates through illusion and desire, and acquire a fresh, spiritual way of thinking." In short, to be holy means to "put on that new man created in God's image, whose justice and holiness are born of truth" (*Ephesians* 4:22-24).

There is only one means to holiness: union with Christ, and this is pure gift. There are many things we can do, with the help of God's grace, to lessen our resistance to receiving this gift, or to foster growth in union with Christ. God doesn't just sweep our human natures aside and make us holy by a one-sided act of power on His part (see above, chapter five). But nothing we do is automatically effective, and no particular exercise of devotion or of asceticism is the "one thing necessary." For God to pour the "new wine" of His holiness, His life, into us He simply has to make us new. And we have to accept that dying and rising, that "going down" (cp. *Matthew* 4:6) into the grave through baptism, in which God makes us new.

This is what Jesus is teaching here: "People do not pour new wine into old wineskins. If they do, the skins burst, the wine spills out, and the skins are ruined. No, they pour new wine into new wineskins, and in that way both are preserved" (9:17).

As "Master of the Way" Jesus is teaching here that we must not put our hope for holiness or salvation in any human practice, exercise or observance as a means for entering into the Kingdom of heaven, but simply in the gift and the power of God. This is supernatural hope.

*The synagogue leader's daughter*

In dispelling the third "temptation" or illusion of this section, Jesus teaches us the undivided love we should have for God.

During His temptations in the desert, Jesus was urged to make a "deal" with the devil (see *Matthew* 4:9). And this is a temptation that all of us, under one form or another, must face. The power of evil is a fact in this world — the power of evil men, evil institutions, evil governments, sociological movements and philosophies. Those in positions of "power and glory" (*Luke* 4:6) are usually able to threaten the well-being of other people, even to the point of menacing life itself. We are naturally tempted to compromise.

The Church herself seems at different times in her history to have entered into a "pact with the devil" in order to survive. One wonders, for example, about the compromises Church leaders made with Hitler. One wonders today about some of the alliances between religion and big business, religious spokesmen and the spokesmen of wealth and power. Caesar is always a force to be reckoned with, and few can stand up to him without fear.

Fear is the tool of the devil. He plays on it, excites it, intensifies it, and uses it to paralyze our hearts. And the greatest fear he uses is the fear of death (see *Hebrews* 2:15). Jesus, on the other hand is constantly preaching against fear (*Matthew* 6:25-34). Fear is useless, He says; what is needed is trust (*Mark* 5:36). He came to rid us of fear (*Luke* 1:74), and He tells us we do not have to live in it (*Luke* 12:32). His messengers introduce themselves by saying, "You have nothing to fear!" (*Luke* 1:30; 2:10). And Jesus makes Himself known in the same way (see *Matthew* 14:27; 17:7; 28:10; *Acts* 18:9). He tells us we should not even fear death itself or those who can inflict death on us. There is only one we should fear: God (*Matthew* 10:28-33), just as there is only one we should adore:

> You shall do homage to the
>    Lord your God;
> him alone shall you adore.

(*Matthew* 4:10; cf. *Exodus* 20:2-6; *Deuteronomy* 6:13)

When Jesus quoted these words during His temptation in the desert, He was with the devil on a

"very high mountain." This scene recalls the occasion
when God first spoke these words to Moses on the top
of Mount Sinai, where He had summoned him to
receive the Ten Commandments (see *Exodus* 19:20;
20:2-6; *Deuteronomy* 5:6-9). In this admonition, however, the ideas of love and fear and worship are used
almost interchangeably. The warning not to adore or
pay homage to any other gods is the same as the
warning not to fear them: "The LORD, your God,
shall you fear; him shall you serve, and by his name
shall you swear" (*Deuteronomy* 6:13). And this is just
an echo of the great commandment of Israel:

> Hear, O Israel! The LORD is our God, the LORD
> alone! Therefore, you shall love the LORD, our God
> with all your heart, and with all your soul, and with
> all your strength. (*Deuteronomy* 6:4-5)

In the measure, then, that we are delivered from
fear, we are free to adore and love the Lord with
undivided hearts, and to serve Him with all our soul.
This was the redemption that was celebrated and
proclaimed by Zechariah at the birth of John the
Baptizer: "that, *rid of fear* and *delivered from the
enemy*, we should serve him devoutly and through all
our days be holy in his sight" (*Luke* 1:74-75).

The synagogue leader whom Matthew presents
to us now as asking Jesus to raise his daughter from
the dead (*Matthew* 9:18) is accepting Jesus as the
Messiah — as the one God has sent to deliver us from
death so that "rid of fear and delivered from the
enemy" we might be able to love and serve God with
"all our heart, all our soul, all our strength."

The tempter, however, appears. This time it takes
the form of scepticism and ridicule. The crowd at the
dead girl's house laugh to scorn the idea that what
appears as death to us is only sleep in the eyes of

God (9:23-24). Paul would encounter the same ridicule later in Athens (*Acts* 17:18, 32; see also 26:24). And as long as they are "making a din" with their instinctual mourning and despair, Jesus can do nothing. He puts them out of the house. Then He takes the little girl by the hand and raises her to her feet.

Was the girl in reality dead, or just unconscious? Matthew leaves it ambiguous and it is not important. The key to the story is that Jesus does in fact deliver us from death, but that we, on our side, have to accept in faith to put aside our fears in order to hear His lifegiving voice. We have to let him "put out" of our house all those tumultuous emotions and instincts within us which make such a din in our minds that we are unable to attend to His words. Once their clamor is silenced we can hear Him calling us to life.

As long as we are "anxious and upset about many things" (*Luke* 10:41) we cannot focus on the Lord with undivided attention. Before Jesus tells us, therefore, to "Seek first the kingdom of God" (an echo of "him alone shall you adore" and "you shall love the Lord with all your heart") He tells us not to worry about the necessities of life on this earth (see *Matthew* 6:19-34). If we have understood that Jesus *is* Life (see above, chapter nine), then we will not succumb to the temptation to divide ourselves, our energies, or our loyalty between Him and other values in this world. And this is what it means to "love the Lord, our God, with all your heart, and with all your soul, and with all your strength." Through Jesus we can love God with an undivided love.

*The two blind men: Jesus is revealed as light*
After His temptations in the desert Matthew tells us that Jesus "withdrew" into Galilee. This was because He heard that John the Baptizer had been

arrested by Herod. It was also, Matthew tells us, a
fulfillment of the prophecy:

"A people living in darkness
    has seen a great light.
On those who inhabit a land
    overshadowed by death,
light has arisen." (*Matthew* 4:16)

Now in chapter nine Matthew shows us Jesus
being in action the light-giver for those in darkness.
He gives sight to the two blind men who cry out to
Him, "Son of David, have pity on us" (9:27-31).

Jesus doesn't cure the two blind men when they
first call out to Him, however. He waits until He
reaches the house to which He was going (9:28).
When they catch up with Him there, apart from the
crowd, He asks them, "Are you confident I can do
this?" When they say they are, He restores their sight.

We see here the Teacher in action. There are
some things Jesus can't teach us — questions He can't
ask us, and words He can't speak to us — in the midst
of a crowd. He has to take us apart and question the
depth of our souls. "What are you looking for? (*John*
1:38). "Are you confident I can do this?" (*Matthew*
9:28). "And you, who do you say that I am?" (*Matthew* 18:15).

It is worth noticing that in Matthew's Gospel the
word "withdraw" has a special significance. Jesus
never "flees" from His enemies, for example; He
"withdraws." And almost every time Matthew uses
this word (in Greek *anachoreo*) in speaking of Jesus,
the context is the same: some opposition to His
mission arises, and He "withdraws" — usually into
greater solitude — in response to it.

In chapter four, after His temptations in the
desert, He "withdraws" into Galilee because John has

been arrested. In chapter twelve, when the Pharisees begin to plot against Him, He withdraws again (*Matthew* 12:15). In chapter fourteen, the news of John's death causes Jesus to withdraw by boat "to a deserted place by himself" (*Matthew* 14:13). And in chapter fifteen, after a heated argument with the Pharisees, He withdraws into Tyre and Sidon, an area more pagan than Jewish (*Matthew* 15:21).

Jesus has no fear of His enemies, and He teaches us not to have fear. When, however, the enemy is active in our lives, He teaches us by His own example to "withdraw." The purpose of this withdrawal is not just to escape; it is to seek or to establish the conditions necessary for us to hear God's voice, to come into the clarity of His light. Our strength comes from our union with God; and our union with God is fostered, among other ways, by prayer. Without prayer we simply will not love and serve the Lord with "all our heart, all our soul, and all our strength." We need prayer in order to love with undivided hearts (see *Matthew* 26:41).

Before Jesus called the synagogue leader's daughter back to life, He had to put out of the house all those whose mourning and carrying-on were making a din. The word Matthew puts in Jesus' mouth when He tells them to leave is *anachoreite*, the word that means "withdraw." And we have already seen the signficance of this for our lives: in order to listen to Jesus with undivided attention, and in order to respond to Him with an undivided heart, we have to command our fears and anxieties to "withdraw." No more than we are able to serve two masters, or give ourselves simultaneously to God and money (*Matthew* 6:24) are we able to follow two teachers or give our attention simultaneously to the voice of our fears and to Jesus.

Our fears blind us. So do other things that set up a clamor in our souls. Jesus taught us in the parable of the sower that what makes us blind and deaf to His teaching and unable to be healed by Him as "Master of the Way" (*Matthew* 13:14-15) is the dividedness of our hearts. We listen to His words, but our "anxieties over life's demands, and the desire for wealth, and cravings of other sorts" (*Mark* 4:19) keep us from really hearing Him or seeing by His light.

If we recognize our blindness, however, and cry out to Him, then He becomes our light. It is Jesus who ordered those who were making a din in the dead girl's house to "withdraw." And when we are unable to cast out our fears and anxieties ourselves, then we must simply cry out to Him as Son of David, "Have pity on us."

Then, if we are willing to be "confident" He can do it, He will make us see.

*The possessed mute*

The last thing Matthew told us about Jesus in his announcement of Him as Savior and "Master of the Way" (*Matthew*, chapters 3-4), is that after John the Baptizer was arrested, Jesus Himself began to call us to conversion (*Matthew* 4:17). And to make clear the nature of this conversion, he tells us that Jesus' first act was to invite four men to leave behind their employment, their means of livelihood, and their social connections and to follow Him (*Matthew* 4:18-22).

Jesus showed by this act that He came to call us to a transcendent destiny: to a relationship with God that transcends all earthly relationships; to a mission and purpose in life that transcends all earthly occupations (see above, chapter two). The disciples left nets, boat and father to follow Him. Jesus promised in return to make them "fishers of men" and sons of His Father in heaven. The conversion He called them to, and calls us to, is not a conversion from evil to good — just to turn away from sins, that is — but from what is humanly good to a participation in the life and activity of God. Jesus is the Teacher, not of good human behavior on earth, but of life on the level of God's own attitudes and values (see, for example, *Matthew* 6:43-48).

He gives us this life by enabling us to speak. This is the significance of the cure of the possessed mute (*Matthew* 9:32-34).

The act most characteristic of God — in His relationship to the world, at least — is creation. God speaks, and the world is made. Whenever He says "Let it be," it is (see *Genesis,* chapter one). The hallmark of divinity is God's creative word. All existence is nothing but His utterance; His breath is the breath of life (*Genesis* 2:7; *Psalms* 33:6-9; and cp. *Matthew* 4:4).

But we are in the image of God (*Genesis* 1:26-27). Our words also are creative — not of external reality around us, but of our own, interior being. We *are* the words we utter: the words, that is, of self-determining choice. Of all the creatures God made, only one is able to answer when God calls him by name. That one is us. And when God calls us to respond to Him we *are* the answer we give.

The problem is, sin has made us mute. We are unable to utter words of response to God, because we are unable even to hear him — at least, to hear Him distinctly. Not only our own sins, but the sins of the world which condition the environment in which we live, and through it condition us, have made us "sluggish of heart." We listen but do not understand;

we look intently and still we know nothing (*Isaiah* 6:9-10). And so we cannot speak. God calls us and we cannot answer. Before His summons to create our souls by words of heroic response — words of free, self-determining choice — we stand mute and inert. Or else we mumble mediochrity.

It isn't by chance that the mute in Matthew's story is also possessed by the devil. His muteness is a muteness of soul. It is not just his tongue that is bound, but his spirit. And so, "once the demon was expelled the mute began to speak" (*Matthew* 9:33).

It is characteristic of God's redemptive action in our lives to free us from whatever inhibits our response. He restores our freedom of choice. He opens our ears to His words, our eyes to the possibilities ahead of us, and our mouths to answer His call. And when we answer, we are free.

The call of Jesus, however, does not just free us to speak our human words again. In the Scriptures, when God intervenes in a person's life and makes him able to speak, it is to deliver a divine message. Moses, for example, was told to deliver God's message to Pharaoh. When he objected, "Please, Lord, I have never been eloquent . . . I am slow of speech and tongue," God responded: "Who gives one man speech and makes another deaf and dumb? Or who gives sight to one and makes another blind? Is it not I, the LORD? Go, then! It is I who will assist you in speaking and will teach you what you are to say" (*Exodus* 4:10-12).

Isaiah likewise, when the Lord wished to send him, lamented: "I am a man of unclean lips." God's answer was to send an angel to touch his mouth with a burning coal from the altar. As the angel did this he said, "See, now that this has touched your lips, your wickedness is removed, your sin purged" (*Isaiah* 6:5-9).

When God makes us able to speak, He releases both lips and heart from bondage. It cannot be otherwise, because our words (of understanding and of choice) are simply the expression of our souls. Jesus said, "The mouth speaks whatever fills the mind ... By your words you will be acquitted, and by your words you will be condemned." (*Matthew* 12:34-37). When Jesus makes us able to speak in His name, then, He purifies our hearts.

This is the significance of Jesus' call to His first disciples in the opening chapters of Matthew. And it is the significance of His cure of the possessed mute in chapter nine. The mission of Jesus is to raise us to a whole new level of existence — the level of God's own life. He does this by summoning us — and empowering us — to speak words of response to God that are beyond the power of man to utter, words that can only be spoken in unison with the Spirit speaking them within us (see *Romans* 8:15; 1 *Corinthians* 12:3; see also *Matthew* 10:19-20). As "Son of David" Jesus not only brings Jewish history to its final peak of fulfillment (see above, chapter two), but He sets before us and calls us to the peak of all human achievement, which is to share in His own life and mission on earth. He sends us to speak in His name, not only with the creative power, by His Spirit, to shape our own souls in His likeness (*Colossians* 3:10; *Philippians* 3:10) but also with redemptive power by the same Spirit to "speak" with Him the new creation of the world (see *Galatians* 4:19-20; *Ephesians* 1:3-23; 4:15-16; *Revelation* 21:1-5).

I call you friends,
since I have made known to

you all that I heard from
my father.
It was not you who chose me,
it was I who chose you
to go forth and bear fruit. (*John* 15:15-16)

The fruit that we bear "in Christ" is a fruit that
will endure. The "words" that we speak in Him are
words of everlasting life; they will never pass away
(cp. *John* 5:63-68 and *Matthew* 34:35). In this we can
see the echo, to us, of the promise God made to David
about his son and heir: "Your house and your kingdom shall endure forever before me; your throne shall
stand firm forever" (2 *Samuel* 7:16). In Him the
"words" that we speak — words of our own self-
determination in grace, and words of healing and life
for others — will give us a voice forever (cp. *Genesis*
15:1-6; 17:1-8).

*Conclusion*

With the story of the possessed mute Matthew
brings to a conclusion the first part of His Gospel, in
which he presents to us the mission and ministry of
Jesus and invites us to respond to Him as saving
presence of God on earth.[2]

At the same time he faces us with our own
"response-ability." We are no longer mute. We are
called upon to speak. And the "words" that we speak
are not just human words: they are words charged
with the creative, redemptive power of Jesus Himself,
whose Body on earth we are. In us and through us it is
Jesus Himself who desires to respond to the needs of
the world. We have the power to let Him do it.

Since we have this "response-ability," we have
the responsibility to use it. And this is what Matthew
calls our attention to in a very subtle way as he closes
the brackets on this section of his Gospel.

We have already seen that Matthew's next sentence after the story of the possessed mute (9:35) is a repeat of an earlier sentence (4:23) in which Matthew introduces us to Jesus being Teacher and Savior in action. After the first use of this sentence, however, Matthew tells us, "They *carried to him* all those afflicted with various diseases and racked with pain... He cured them all. The great crowds that followed him came from Galilee, the Ten Cities, Jerusalem and Judea, and from across the Jordan" (4:24-25).

The second time Matthew gives us this sentence, he follows it with the statement:

> At the sight of the crowds, his heart was moved with pity. They were lying prostrate from exhaustion, like sheep without a shepherd.

Jesus sees it is not possible for them all to come to Him. They are too many, and they are too far gone in apathy and disillusionment. They have ceased to hope. Nor is there anyone to lead them to Him. They are like sheep without a shepherd; left to themselves, they will just stay where they are until they die.

The answer is that He must go to them. If they cannot, will not, come to Him from all the corners of the world — not just from "Galilee, the Ten Cities, Jerusalem and Judea, and from across the Jordan," but from every culture and corner of the earth — then he must go out to them. And so He said to His disciples, "The harvest is good but laborers are scarce. Beg the harvest master to *send out* laborers to gather his harvest" (*Matthew* 9:36-38).

With that statement Matthew changes the focus from Jesus alone to Jesus in union with His Church. The Word that was made flesh in Jesus must now be made flesh in His whole Body on earth. And in that

Body the Word that was spoken in Jesus will continue to be spoken until the end of time. The power of the devil has been broken. The first Adam, after his sin, was afraid to respond to God's voice (see *Genesis* 3:9-10). In the new Adam, who has delivered us from sin; mankind will never be mute again, but will answer, "Here I am!" (see *Isaiah* 6:8; see also *Genesis* 26:2; *Exodus* 3:4; 1 *Samuel* 3:4; *Judith* 9:6; *Acts* 9:10).

### FOOTNOTES

[1]See my book *The Good News About Sex*, ch. 11: "Sex As Symbolic Language," for an explanation of spousal love as a commitment to achieving union of mind and heart and will (St. Anthony Messenger Press, 1979).

[2]With this same passage Matthew also opens the "brackets" on another block of material, which deals with the mission and ministry of the *Church* (see Matthew 12:22). But that is not a topic for us to deal with here.

CHAPTER THIRTEEN: JESUS IS TEACHER OF LIFE —
*Matthew*, chapter nine

*Summary:*

1. The ending of the Gadara story (8:33-34) and the cure of the paralytic at Capernaum (9:1-8) both show Jesus *calling us to conversion.* He doesn't just heal the body; He addresses the heart. He summons us to choose. And in the act of choosing we either open ourselves or close ourselves to the *experience of God* and of our relatedness to Him.

2. In the next three incidents, as during His temptations in the desert (*Matthew* 4:1-11), Jesus *corrects misconceptions* about the nature of His mission and of the religion He teaches. Through the call of Matthew and His association with sinners (9:9-13), Jesus shows us that *life*, not the Law, is the goal of His religion. *Faith*, and not legalism, is the key to relationship with Him.

   In His answer to John's disciples (9:14-17), Jesus makes clear that the *means* to salvation are not really to be found in what we do, but in one thing only: union with Him. Jesus Himself is our salvation and life, and to be "holy" simply means to be one with Him. We must put our *hope*, then, not in practices and observances (no matter how good they might be), but simply in Him, and in the favor of union with Him, which is "grace."

The raising of the synagogue leader's daughter (9:18-26) is Christ's answer to the idolatry of a divided heart. We cannot serve God with our whole hearts if we are fragmented by *fear*. Fear inclines us to compromise with evil. Jesus delivers us from fear by overcoming death, which is the root of all our fears. The religion of Jesus is a religion of *undivided love*.

3. The cures of the two blind men (9:27-31) and of the possessed mute (9:32-34) are a final *revelation of Christ's identity*. Matthew shows Him again as the light (cp. 4:12-16) and the life (cp. 4:17-22) of the world. The blind men give Him His title: "Son of David." And He empowers the mute to speak. True life is to *know God* by the supernatural light of faith and to *respond* to God with "words" of love and self-creating choice. Jesus, who is the Word of God made flesh, came that we might have life in re-uttering with the Father the "word" of His name in love. When we utter His name by grace, we are at the same time speaking and determining our own.

*Questions for prayer and discussion:*

1. In what way has Jesus called me to conversion? What have I personally chosen to change in my life because of encounter with Him? How did this encounter take place?

2. Can I relate my experience of God to my acts of free choice in response to Christ? When and how have I known most deeply that God is real to me?

3. What do I really aim at in my religion? Keeping out of sin, or getting to know Christ better? In what do I place my confidence for salvation? In my religious observances, or just in what I know Jesus is and chooses to be for me? How much does fear determine my choices? What, concretely, do I fear so much that it makes me compromise in my response to the Gospel?

4. This chapter invites me to *discipleship*; that is, to a decision to *learn* from Jesus as "Master of the Way". In what concrete ways am I trying to learn from Him now? What will I do, or continue to do, in order to be in a real and significant way His disciple? Why?

## EPILOGUE

We began this book asking, "Why Jesus?" We end it asking, "Why me?"

It is impossible to encounter Jesus Christ without encountering ourselves. As we see what Jesus can be — wants to be, offers to be — for us, each one of us must ask, not "What do I want Jesus to be for me? but "What do I want to be for Him? — for other people? for the world? What do I want to be for me?"

How much do I value my existence? What do I want it to be? How do I want to use it? The answers I give to these questions are the answer I make to the question "Why me?"

The answer is not academic. What I answer is what I will be.

It is when we answer that question, and try to answer it seriously, that we come to appreciate what Jesus really is.

Why Jesus?

Because He is the only satisfactory answer to the question, "Why me?"